Entrepreneurship in the Wild

Entrepreneurship in the Wild

A STARTUP FIELD GUIDE

Felipe G. Massa

The MIT Press
Cambridge, Massachusetts
London, England

The MIT Press would like to thank the anonymous peer reviewers who provided comments on drafts of this book. The generous work of academic experts is essential for establishing the authority and quality of our publications. We acknowledge with gratitude the contributions of these otherwise uncredited readers.

This book was set in Stone Serif by Westchester Publishing Services. Printed and bound in the United States of America.

Library of Congress Cataloging-in-Publication Data

Names: Massa, Felipe G., author.
Title: Entrepreneurship in the wild : a startup field guide / Felipe G. Massa.
Description: Cambridge : The MIT Press, 2021. | Includes bibliographical
    references and index.
Identifiers: LCCN 2020036748 | ISBN 9780262542579 (paperback)
Subjects: LCSH: New business enterprises. | Industrial management. |
    Strategic planning.
Classification: LCC HD62.5 .M36567 2021 | DDC 658.1/1--dc23
LC record available at https://lccn.loc.gov/2020036748

10 9 8 7 6 5 4 3 2 1

I dedicate this book to my mother, my favorite entrepreneur and superhero

Contents

Welcome

By cracking open this book you have taken a meaningful step toward making a mark in your community. You have gone from being an employee, a student, or a part-timer to becoming a founder. Founders stand apart because they brazenly declare they will forge a path that others will follow. There are no special plaques or ceremonies needed for someone to become a founder, no entry fees or golden tickets. Instead, founders need a commitment to persevere and learn from challenges large and small.[1] The process of launching a startup is energizing and filled with limitless potential, something no job can match. It is an opportunity to shape a new, brighter future. Many founders, however, stumble when they try to turn their imagined future into a tangible reality.[2] They might have all the fervor needed to start a business but not know where to focus their energy. They might have extraordinary skills but no experience applying these skills in the startup context. The result is often frustration and, eventually, a failed venture.

This book will help founders launch their startup in a way that wastes less time and consumes fewer resources. Instead of suggesting a "field of dreams"[3] strategy—whereby a founder launches a startup and hopes people will magically show up—it embraces a systematic approach that is a lot less taxing than haphazard trial-and-error approaches and a lot more likely to lead to **traction.**[*] It capitalizes on emerging experiential or action-based[4] approaches to entrepreneurship education that couple learning by doing with the important work of familiarizing oneself with essential concepts, relevant examples, and tools needed to put lessons into practice as soon as possible. Entrepreneurs who

---

[*]According to veteran startup mentor and investor Martin Zwilling in "How Much Traction Is Enough for Investors?" (2013), "Traction is evidence that your product or service has started that 'hockey-stick' adoption rate which implies a large market, a valid business model and sustainable growth. Investors want evidence that the 'dogs are eating the dog food,' and your financial projections are not just a dream" (see https://www.entrepreneur.com/article/225902.).

follow this approach are immersed in the activity of starting a business and are guided by the dual goal of successfully developing their startup and understanding the principles underlying successful entrepreneurship. This book details this systematic approach over the course of ten chapters, each demanding hands-on effort from founders, from the initial foray into generating an idea to the meticulous crafting of a pitch designed to inspire external audiences.

It is important to note that this book does not do the work for you. Instead, it helps you understand when you have done too little or when it is time to move on. It pushes you to feel more confident in the steps you are taking as you advance through what may feel like an unfamiliar and untamed wilderness. Hence the title, *Entrepreneurship in the Wild: A Startup Field Guide*. I find the metaphor of the explorer braving the wilderness appropriate for founders launching startups, for many reasons. They must venture forth, charting new paths while avoiding traps and overcoming challenges. They must also navigate using the tools and practices developed by their predecessors who succeeded in starting businesses and the lessons learned by those who failed. That is why, unlike a traditional textbook, this book is designed as a field guide that uses the language of way-finding. The process of wayfinding involves four discrete stages that apply as easily to the wilderness of **startup ecosystems**[†] as to the navigation of a neglected nature trail.[5] I use the four stages as guideposts to organize each chapter and keep you on track:

- **Orientation** is the attempt to determine one's location relative to objects that may be nearby and the desired destination. We begin every chapter with a short case study and an introduction intended to orient founders as to their location relative to that of other founders who have had similar experiences.

- **Route decision** entails the selection of a course to a destination. The book guides founders through a series of steps designed both to convey important entrepreneurship principles and to advance a founder's progress in the entrepreneurial process. Following these steps, founders will make decisions about how to proceed in establishing their startup.

- **Route monitoring** involves checking to make sure that the selected route is heading toward the destination. In each chapter, as founders reach milestones, they are asked to reflect on and conduct due diligence regarding their decisions.

- **Destination recognition** occurs when an important milestone is reached and new itineraries can be undertaken. In this stage, founders consider what they have accomplished and think carefully about any additional steps they might take before moving on to the next step. Every chapter provides references to external resources and time-tested advice that will help you do just that.

[†] Startup or entrepreneurial ecosystems consist of individuals and organizations that work in concert to support entrepreneurship in a particular space or place. The concept is used by scholars and practitioners to understand value creation by a community or a business, investors, professionals, policymakers, and others in a geographic area or context.

Is This Book Right for Me?

This book targets a broad audience of aspiring entrepreneurs and entrepreneurship educators looking for an accessible, structured approach to new venture development. For more than eight years, the content of the book has been tested by undergraduate, graduate, and executive program students. It has been used and reused by entrepreneurs who lack the structure of a formal startup development program but who wish to try their hand at launching a business. It has also been useful to serial entrepreneurs who have a lot of experience starting businesses but who want to approach the process in a more intentional and measured way.

The tools provided in this book are not exclusively for founders; they can also be deployed by innovators who have no intention of starting their own business and prefer instead to use the entrepreneurial process to bolster a corporate innovation project or build support for organizational change. Even though the book's lexicon and cases focus on the founder's experience, most of the tools provided are agnostic as to whether you are the person starting the business or a change agent helping develop an existing business.

This book is not, however, for people who want advice on how to scale up their startup *after* receiving investment. The book guides entrepreneurs through the process *leading up to* your pitch to investors and does not cover the ins and outs of day-to-day management of a new business or the process of expanding beyond a single market. It is also not designed to be a single source of information for those starting a business. Throughout the book I encourage founders to immerse themselves in their local entrepreneurial ecosystem and to read broadly.

Why Now?

The idea for this book was born several years ago when I was searching for a textbook to adopt for an entrepreneurship class. I wanted to design a class that was as hands-on as possible and that would allow students to experience, in a grounded and research-supported way, what it was like to launch their own venture. Unfortunately, there were few books out there that balanced pragmatic, experiential approaches with more academically rigorous content. I decided to forgo assigning a textbook and built a class out of articles and a set of worksheets I wrote myself. By writing the materials myself, I could be sure that the content was as up-to-date and empirically validated as possible while still being useful to people starting very different types of businesses, ranging from non-profits to high-growth startups. Reflecting the impetus for its creation, this book is not as comprehensive or as involved as a textbook and is not as light on empirical support as many of the practitioner-oriented books in the market. It's designed to be ideal for my own experiential approach to teaching, for startup incubators that can't offer full semester classes, and for people who want to experiment with starting a business but don't want to commit to a full course of study in entrepreneurship. This book is also different from other websites, blogs, and books that are available to aspiring entrepreneurs, for a variety of reasons:

- The approach taken in this book is systematic and, whenever possible, empirically supported. It is not, however, bounded by any one school of thought or dominating discourse on how one might start a business today. I draw as heavily on lean startup principles as I do on the "jobs-to-be-done" framework, on the fundamentals of design thinking, and on findings in the entrepreneurship literature that are not available in paperback yet. I believe this approach is ideal because I find the weaknesses of any one method tend to be balanced out by the strengths of another.

- Instead of creating a stand-alone book and a separate workbook, I have chosen to create an all-in-one solution that I believe fits well with how founders prefer to engage in new venture development. As such, I ask that founders create their own startup in manageable sprints that follow immediately after rich examples and explanations. If you have an extra hour or two here and there, you will be able to make progress. I also supplement the book with online resources available on the MIT Press website (https://mitpress.mit.edu/massa-wild) that were crafted to make learning the entrepreneurial process and teaching it easier. Because resources are available online, they can be updated often, and so are more likely to reflect current best practices.

- Instead of overwhelming founders with theory and in-depth explanations of each concept I introduce in the book, I give readers a choice. By engaging with the footnotes and works cited at the end of the book, readers can access primary and secondary sources that inform what I write. If, however, founders are already comfortable with or uninterested in concepts and theories, they can ignore the small type and focus on the work of getting a startup off the ground. Entrepreneurship is an unapologetically practical discipline that, through the work of dedicated researchers, has gained scholarly grounding. It is up to you whether you want to dig deeper into the exciting research being generated by scholars all over the world.

- Finally, this book takes a cue from Steve Case, cofounder of AOL, and his Rise of the Rest campaign.[6] Cases at the beginning of each chapter in this book feature entrepreneurs living and working outside the Silicon Valley bubble—in some instances in poor communities, where they may lack access to startup financing.[7] Moreover, several of the featured entrepreneurs are women and people of color, who have historically been excluded from educational experiences and from mentorship and the financial support networks that bolster startup success rates.[8] The result is a book that is grounded in real success stories lived by real people in cities and towns across America.

How to Use This Book

I expect you to have gotten some mileage out of this book by the time you are done with it. Write in the margins, fill in the blank spaces with thoughts and ideas, and rip out pages to take with you to a founding team meeting. If you are reading the e-book, download worksheets that match each chapter from the MIT Press website (https://mitpress.mit .edu/massa-wild). And if you start another business, buy a new book or download more worksheets. This is not a ploy to sell more books but an invitation to really engage with the content in as active and visceral a way as possible. This book is valuable only insofar as it is used to advance your startup. Do not put the knowledge in the book on a pedestal, put it to the test.

Jump in, have fun, and create something meaningful!

Ideas with Legs

Objectives

- Identify opportunities in a customer's jobs to be done.
- Synthesize elegant solutions that fit pressing jobs to be done.
- Conduct due diligence to ensure your idea captures customer interest and has sizable upside potential.
- Craft a compelling positioning statement that conveys the value of your solution to early customers, experts, and investors.

1.1 Mini Case: The Rise of Bagel Boy

While working at a bagel shop in New Orleans, Brendan Dodd noticed that at the end of slow days, leftover bagels would be thrown away. He asked his manager whether he could take the leftover bagels home and give them to his friends. Strapped for both cash and time as they balanced college classes and part-time jobs, his friends eagerly gobbled up the day-old bagels. After a while, bringing bagels home and giving them away became routine: "I started to post on Facebook to see if any of my friends wanted any. If anyone claimed a bagel, I would just hop on my bike to deliver it. It was a good way to get exercise and to see my friends. One day a friend called me Bagel Boy, and the name just stuck." The owners of the bagel shop where Brendan worked were happy that the bagels were not going to waste, so he kept going. After he posted about the bagels on a collegewide Facebook group, demand grew quickly, far outpacing the supply of leftovers from the bagel shop. Brendan started to wonder whether some of the people claiming the free bagels would be willing to pay for them, particularly since many of them had started to tip him for delivery. By chatting with people he delivered bagels to and with people claiming bagels online, he came to realize that (1) there was a lot of unmet demand for bagels in other parts of the city and (2) people who were working full-time really cared more about the convenience his deliveries provided than the fact that they were free.

Brendan knew that selling bagels could be easy if he put together the right business model and reached customers where and how they wanted to be reached: "Some of the neighborhoods in New Orleans were really underserved because almost all the bagel shops were uptown." Word of mouth from Brendan's delivery customers and successful postings on Facebook attracted the attention of local coffee shops, which reached out, asking for wholesale prices. After looking at profit margins for deliveries, Brendan decided to continue serving individuals who ordered online to keep feeding word-of-mouth, but at the same time to focus on expanding his footprint in the more profitable and stable wholesale business. Serving these businesses while limiting direct, low-volume orders would also make deliveries to different parts of the city possible with a small staff.

Just to make sure he was not reading the market incorrectly, Brendan reached out to some of the businesses he thought might make good customers. He targeted coffee shops in neighborhoods that seemed well represented in his Facebook group and were not currently served by a local bagel shop. The response was very positive—in fact, some of the coffee shops were ready to put in orders. Once he was sure he could close enough wholesale deals to support himself, Brendan decided to incorporate, put together a rudimentary website, rent time in a commercial kitchen, and begin making his own bagels. A couple of years after he first began delivering free bagels to his friends, and a few tweaks to the business model later, Bagel Boy and his growing staff were making and delivering bulk orders of fresh bagels and spreads every day to dozens of coffee shops and loyal customers all over New Orleans.

1.2   Orientation: Generating Ideas

A major challenge founders face is the struggle to generate viable ideas for a new venture. Even the most successful serial entrepreneurs hope their idea will spark excitement for the founding team, investors, and, most important, potential customers. When idealism and a passion for innovation do not elicit inspiration or gain traction with customers, one of two things tends to happen: either (1) the lack of traction becomes a source of frustration that dissuades otherwise creative and hard-working individuals from pursuing entrepreneurship, or (2) after losing confidence, the founder launches a venture like others in the immediate area—yet another restaurant or shop that seems like a safe bet but that faces endless competition—which often leads to a startup's quick demise.

In either case, the founder loses interest, loses motivation, or loses money. As the adage goes, an aspiring entrepreneur without a compelling business idea to pursue is just a dreamer with an expensive hobby. This chapter avoids assuming readers already have a great idea when they decide to try their hand at entrepreneurship. As the Bagel Boy case illustrates, the idea generation process often involves little bets* on hunches that

---

*Small-scale experimentation (or "little bets") allow innovators to try new ideas with low failure costs but potentially large rewards. Peter Sims in *Little Bets: How Breakthrough Ideas Emerge from Small Discoveries* (New

assume the shape of a full-fledged business idea only through the founder's experiences and interactions with potential customers and experts that help founders "connect the dots"[†] or identify important patterns in consumer behavior. Rushing through the idea generation process will yield uninspired ideas that lack a solid foundation.

This chapter is designed to increase the likelihood that the idea underlying your venture is feasible and actionable. It offers a structured series of iterative steps that help you identify an idea that has legs, that is, an idea that has the potential to survive the gauntlet of feedback and changing market dynamics that are part and parcel of entrepreneurship. In line with recent research on idea generation processes, we suggest you engage with these iterative steps independently at first before brainstorming with or involving other team members.[‡] Instead, reach beyond your immediate social circle and talk to people who you think might resemble either a potential customer or an expert in the field you are entering. Even if you already have in mind an idea you are sure is a winner, completing the steps that follow will help you sharpen your focus and communicate the idea in a compelling way.

1.3   Step 1: Identifying Gaps

Many founders capitalize on ideas born out of their own life experiences, needs, and desires.[1] Some experts mention how good ideas emerge from problems or "pain points" that are not currently being addressed and that someone would pay to have solved.[2] Paul Graham, founder of Y Combinator, an incubator that seeded Airbnb and Dropbox, suggests that "the way to get startup ideas is not to try to think of startup ideas. It's to look for problems, preferably problems you have yourself."[3] The alternative yields what he suggests are dangerously bad ideas that sound just plausible enough to fool you into working on them. Instead of looking for problems or pain points, some founders look at the gains or benefits that might come from adopting a product or service. Whether you follow the glass half full or glass half empty approach is, however, largely immaterial as long as you are able to pinpoint some gap that gives you an opening, that is, a good chance to convince customers to change their current behavior (i.e., to quit using other solutions and buy what you are selling). Customers satisfied with the status quo are

---

York: Simon and Schuster, 2011) notes that Amazon developed its very profitable and scalable Associates program, which rewards other websites for sending buyers to Amazon, using the same trial-and-error method that comedian Chris Rock uses to hone his stand-up routine. The key is to experiment deliberately and leverage limited resources.

[†]Entrepreneurs who come up with compelling ideas tend "connect the dots" between changes in technology, demographics, markets, government policies, and other factors. The patterns they perceive in these events or trends suggest ideas for new products or services—ideas that can potentially serve as the basis for new ventures.

[‡]Founders who work on ideas independently before sharing or brainstorming in a team setting structure can generate more ideas, generate better ideas, and better discern the quality of the ideas they generate. The frequently recommended brainstorming technique of building on others' ideas is counterproductive. Teams exhibiting such buildup do not create more ideas, nor are the ideas that build on previous ideas better. Karan Girotra, Christian Terwiesch, and Karl T. Ulrich, "Idea Generation and the Quality of the Best Idea," *Management Science* 56, no. 4 (2010): 591–605.

unlikely to experiment with new solutions or even to consider searching for a new way to do things; they have no reason to do so. So, if you are selling a benefit that does not address a specific, known problem, you must first convince customers to consider spending time and money on a solution to a problem they didn't realize they had.

When trying to come up with a good idea that exploits a gap, you might begin by formulating questions that help you identify a situation a customer perceives as suboptimal:

- Can you think of instances in which you or someone you know became frustrated with a product or service?

- Are you knowledgeable about a specific industry that could benefit from a new mode of doing things? Is the current mode less than ideal in some significant way?

- Can you identify improvements or changes you think might make others engage with a service or product more seamlessly?

- Can you draw on your experiences in a job or at school to come up with a problem that, if addressed, could make customers' lives easier and a solution they would be willing to pay for?

As you jot down a few ideas and recall moments of frustration or insight, your hunches may start becoming less fuzzy, or you might reach dead ends. If you are not feeling particularly inspired, try taking a break, going for a walk,[4] or chatting with others about their own concerns and what things they would pay to improve. You will also need downtime to reflect on and process your conversations, integrating your original insights with those you are confronted with as your ideas develop. Good ideas often come from a "collision of hunches"[§] generated by people invested in trying to explore opportunities together, not from the musings of a lone genius.[5] Many founding teams participate in **brainstorming**[¶] sessions both to ensure they have captured as many good ideas as possible and to get all team members on the same page.[6] As you go through this process, whether by yourself or as part of a team, do your best to avoid trivial problems or subtle gains in efficiency. It is easy to become captivated by minutiae. Instead, be sure you are looking for gaps that are pressing, **"tier 1" concerns**—those that are top-of-mind for potential customers and that they want resolved immediately.[7]

[§]Steven Johnson in *Where Good Ideas Come From* (New York: Penguin, 2011) suggests that although we may find the figure of the lone genius captivating, it is often the case that the inventions or paradigm shifting ideas introduced by geniuses don't emerge in the vacuum and are seldom the result of their individual effort.

[¶]Brainstorming was originally developed by Alex Osborn, an advertising executive in the 1940s, as a way of quickly generating multiple creative ideas. He recognized that coming up with good ideas requires two activities, generating and judging. Judging ideas as they are generated can obstruct the creative process and inhibit the kind of out-of-the-box thinking needed to wow clients. "Groupthink" or peer pressure whereby people in the session are reluctant to share ideas for fear of ridicule might even take over. That is why Osborn suggested that ideas should not be judged until the end of a brainstorming session after all individual contributions have been exhausted. Academic research has largely supported Osborn's assertions, adding that while creators working alone tend to create more ideas, working in groups shortens the length of the combined generating and judging process. A. F. Osborn, *Applied Imagination: Principles and Procedures of Creative Problem Solving*, 3rd ed. (New York: Charles Scribner's Sons, 1963).

Brainstorming is a structured ideation process that you have probably participated in at some point in your life. Few groups, however, follow rules to ensure that ideas flow freely and that the best possible idea comes out on top. After nominating a facilitator charged with writing down ideas and keeping contributions orderly, the group should ensure the following:

- Those involved in brainstorming should avoid criticizing emerging ideas, even if they sound silly. Silly ideas may provide a launching point for insight.
- Group members should verbalize all their ideas as they think of them, without fear of criticism. The goal is to generate as many ideas as possible without exercising self-censorship with respect to the perceived quality or worthiness of the ideas.
- Group members are encouraged to combine other ideas into their own and to build on the ideas of others and develop those ideas further.
- Group members should agree as a group that all ideas generated are owned commonly by all those in the group.

If you follow these guidelines and try to have some fun with the process, the ideas you come up with should be more appealing than what you could come up with by yourself. Most important, however, is that brainstorming, when done correctly, can make team members feel involved and appreciated.

An intuitive way to frame this search for tier 1 concerns is to state a gap in terms of what Clayton Christensen and colleagues call the "**job to be done**."[8] With an understanding of the "job" for which customers want to "hire" a product or service, founders can more accurately develop solutions tailored to what customers are already trying to do. For example, no one needs an automated pressure cooker (a product/solution), but busy, time-constrained people do need a way to *prepare food faster and with less mess* (the job to be done). No one needs a *staircase* (a product/solution); they need a *safe and efficient way to reach the second floor* (the job to be done).

Action: Let us try something interactive to get the ideas flowing and to put some of the concepts we have discussed into practice. State three distinct ideas as jobs to be done that are distinct and pressing enough (tier 1) on their own to be considered a reason for starting a new business. That is, do not try to come up with a single business that tackles three jobs; that would be too much for a single, early-stage business. Instead, come up with three significant jobs that you think need to be tackled by a business you would be willing to put together. Match each job to a type of customer who you think might pay for it to get done. For instance, the customer for the automated pressure cooker I mentioned previously might be a busy parent. Try to balance being both detailed and straightforward in your descriptions so that even people not familiar with industry jargon or who are hearing about the idea for the first time could easily understand what you are talking about. Remember: if you are having trouble coming up with three jobs to be done, try asking a friend or a stranger to serve as a sounding board for your ideas.

1. Enter the FIRST job to be done and the customer for whom it is salient here:

```



```

2. Enter the SECOND job to be done and the customer for whom it is salient here:

```



```

3. Enter the THIRD job to be done and the customer for whom it is salient here:

```



```

1.4   Step 2: Matching Jobs to Elegant Solutions

The jobs to be done you just identified are potential **opportunities**.[9] Opportunities come into being when there is legitimate interest on the part of a group of customers to fill a gap or tackle a job to be done. The founders of Uber noticed that existing taxi services suffered from significant problems: cabs were hard to hail, and customers did not feel safe exchanging cash with drivers.[10] These problems were individually frustrating enough for customers to dread taking a taxi. This "pain" suffered because the job was not being done properly and the availability of a well-marketed alternative compelled customers to try ride-sharing services. In the Bagel Boy case, we saw customers openly expressing their desire for more convenient access to fresh bagels. Brendan Dodd identified this as the job to be done and then realized that by selling to coffee shops, he could tackle that job and increase traffic for local businesses (another job to be done) while not having to incur the costs of door-to-door delivery. In this step of the idea generation process, you are going to create solutions that fit the jobs to be done that you generated in the previous step. There are two key tensions you will need to attend to and balance before you list solutions:

- **Tension 1: Focused, yet Scalable.** In starting a new business, you don't need to tackle jobs for a large subset of potential customers, just for a subset that is large enough to sustain your business initially (for one to three years). For instance, when they introduced the personal computer, Microsoft's founders created a solution that would appeal to early adopters of the product (i.e., technologically savvy males who had an interest in programming and enough income to purchase what was then a very expensive machine). This customer segment was not large enough to support Microsoft's business plan in the long run, but it was very excited about the product and would be a good "**beachhead**"** for subsequent marketing efforts.[11] The company's founders recognized early on that a generic solution would not engage the customer. This is because a solution designed to satisfy the whims of a large, heterogeneous grouping of people with different priorities and preferences likely will not satisfy, much less "wow." Remember, as a startup you must disrupt existing habits and be remarkable enough to get a core group of customers to advocate for your product.[12] For the cash-strapped startup, word of mouth is key! At the same time, founders must think about how, after they capture their beachhead, they might scale up their efforts or expand to profitable adjacent markets without completely reinventing their solution or brand. It might be useful to think of this balancing act as if it were a chess game: every piece you move into place will commit you to a path, opening up new alternatives and closing down others. As such, you need to imagine what the game will look like a few moves ahead to ensure that the move you make now (capturing the initial beachhead market) will not prevent you from making important moves in the future (moving into a market that allows your business to grow quickly and meet investor expectations).

- **Tension 2: Satisfying, Not Overwhelming.** It is crucial that your solution address the job to be done in a substantive way. Half solutions or near misses will not thrill customers. If you alleviate a problem only slightly or if your solution generates other problems,

---

** A beachhead market can be defined as a niche market with specific characteristics that make it an ideal target to sell a novel solution. According to Bill Aulet in *Disciplined Entrepreneurship* (Hoboken, NJ: Wiley, 2013), three conditions make a customer segment an ideal beachhead: (1) the customers within the market all buy similar products; (2) the customers within the market have a similar sales cycle and expect products to provide value in similar ways; and (3) word-of-mouth communication exists between customers in the market.

you will not attract sustained customer interest or word of mouth. At the same time, you do not want to try to solve too many problems all at once, particularly if they are not naturally related in the customers' minds. The balance here is between leaving the customer satisfied with the solution but not overwhelmed with myriad features or confused about what job to be done is being addressed.

Action: Come up with three job solution sets. That is, for each of the three distinct jobs to be done listed in the previous step, come up with ONE solution (e.g., a product or service) that tackles it. This solution can be technological (e.g., a device, a website, an app), it can be a new way to deliver value (e.g., Bagel Boy's wholesale business, which didn't require much by way of technology), or a combination of both. Try to limit your description of the solution to each job to two or three sentences. If it takes more to describe the solution, chances are you are probably trying to do too much! In short, the solution to your job to be done should be as elegant[††] as you can make it.

1. Enter your solution for the FIRST job to be done here:

2. Enter your solution for the SECOND job to be done here:

[††] In mathematical problem solving, the solution to a problem (such as a proof of a mathematical theorem) is considered elegant if it is surprisingly simple and insightful yet effective and constructive.

3. Enter your solution for the THIRD job to be done here:

1.5 Route Monitoring: Confirming Your Idea's Potential

In the previous step, I urged you to think about viable solutions to real customer jobs to be done that balance two key tensions. To help you narrow down which ideas will be most likely to capture customer interest and also have sizable upside potential, it is important to examine each job solution set carefully by asking and answering the following questions. If you were careful in the previous steps, you may already have thought through many of these issues. If not, let this step serve as a filter:

- **Urgency:** Would a customer pay to have this job tackled right now in the way you suggest? Without a targeted set of customers whose needs you are addressing well and who urgently need a solution, you might never achieve a stable revenue source. If you find that your solution might not be compelling enough to separate customers from their money now, you might want to go back to the drawing board or tweak the idea to make it more appealing.

- **Scalability:** Is the potential solution to this problem scalable? Can it grow enough to attract investors (if that is your goal)? Is it so specific to a small market that expansion beyond that market is not conceivable with minimal changes? That is, could the business you are proposing grow to become a large company, or is this more of a lifestyle business, such as a mom-and-pop restaurant? If you find that your solution will be hard to grow or that it can only grow enough to support you and a few of your friends (e.g., a bar, a small restaurant, a small website design shop), I urge you to consider whether you want a small business or a scalable, repeatable business that attracts investment.[‡‡]

- **Profitability:** Are the profit margins in the sector you are joining high enough to allow you room to make some early mistakes? Grocery stores, for instance, make very little money

---

[‡‡] A note for people trying to learn as much as possible: if you focus on a small, lifestyle business, you will miss out on learning how to pitch your idea to investors and how to win funding in pitch competitions. If you are using this book for a class, you will maximize learning by dreaming big.

from each transaction they process and require large **economies of scale**[§§] to make the kinds of profits that attract investors. In the Bagel Boy example, we see Brendan opt to sell his bagels directly to businesses that can order in bulk rather than continue selling exclusively to folks interested in eating the bagels because selling in bulk would allow higher margins per sale. The choice to narrow the types of customer one targets early on to ensure profitability is often made by small operators with limited resources.

- **Actionability:** Is someone without rare expertise or endless capital capable of executing an early version of this idea? Would it require the creation of a novel technology that could be years away and would require a huge research-and-development budget? If you find that it would take years and millions to make your idea happen, you might be overreaching a bit. For instance, if your product requires inventing a new technology, such as a new chemical bonding process, that may or may not actually be possible, you might want to reconsider. If it requires just creating an app or a website, on the other hand, you will probably be able to find developers who can help you out. Understanding your own capabilities and a time horizon for success are key at this juncture.

- **Originality:** Is this idea relatively played out or are customers still short on solutions like yours? The last thing you want is to find out after several months of work that someone else has already addressed this gap for the customers you were targeting. Make sure you search thoroughly for competitors, and list how their product or service is different from or similar to yours. If you are designing an app, make sure you visit Apple and Google app stores and search for comparable solutions. Act as if you were your own future customer searching for potential solutions online. Do these available solutions tackle the same job? If so, how do you tackle it in a better way for your customer? Other resources to check include Crunchbase (https://www.crunchbase.com) and AngelList (https://angel.co). Both are active databases listing startups that may be working on solving similar problems or serving similar customer bases.

- **Marketability:** Is the market you are entering a good setting to start a business of the kind you are proposing? Is it a shrinking, mature market or a market that is growing quickly? Startups tend to have a better chance of succeeding in markets where "the pie" is growing quickly. Have a lot of companies been started in this space recently? Is the number of customers in the segment you are targeting growing?

Action: Examine each of your job solution sets carefully and enter them into table 1.1, scoring them from 1 (weak) to 5 (strong) according to their urgency for potential customers, scalability, profitability, actionability, the originality of your idea, and its marketability.

[§§] Economies of scale are the cost advantages that ventures obtain as a result of their scale of operation, with cost per unit of output decreasing with increasing scale. The greater the quantity of output produced, the lower the per-unit fixed cost will be.

Table 1.1 Solution Ranking

	Solution 1					Solution 2					Solution 3				
	Weak————Strong					Weak————Strong					Weak————Strong				
Urgency	1	2	3	4	5	1	2	3	4	5	1	2	3	4	5
Scalability	1	2	3	4	5	1	2	3	4	5	1	2	3	4	5
Profitability	1	2	3	4	5	1	2	3	4	5	1	2	3	4	5
Actionability	1	2	3	4	5	1	2	3	4	5	1	2	3	4	5
Originality	1	2	3	4	5	1	2	3	4	5	1	2	3	4	5
Marketability	1	2	3	4	5	1	2	3	4	5	1	2	3	4	5
Total	Enter sum here					Enter sum here					Enter sum here				

If you find major issues in any of these categories, I suggest you tweak your ideas or go back to the drawing board. Remember, entrepreneurship is an iterative process that will require engaging in continuous trial-and-error exercises. Better to work through issues now than when money and careers are on the line.

1.6 Step 3: Crafting a Positioning Statement

After completing the previous step, select your two highest-ranking ideas. In my classes, I ask students to rework any ideas that do not exceed twenty points in the due diligence exercise. I find that low scores tend to make the rest of the new venture development process challenging. It is also important, however, that you really care about putting in the work to make these ideas happen. Make certain these are jobs you are passionate about tackling and the solutions are ones you believe in. Could you pursue this idea within the next few years? Would you want to?

Action: Using all the information you have gathered thus far, write positioning statements in tables 1.2 and 1.3 for two ideas that passed the due diligence assessment. A **positioning statement** is a concise description of your beachhead market and should deliver a compelling picture of how you want customers in that market to perceive your solution.[13] Though it may read like promotional materials, your positioning statement can be used as an internal tool. Every product and marketing decision you make regarding your business should align with and support your positioning statement. A good positioning statement helps you maintain focus on your brand and its value proposition while you work on a sensible go-to-market strategy.

PRIMARY IDEA:

Table 1.2 Positioning Statement

For (clear description target customer segment):
who (have the following job to be done):
our (product/service name):
is a (type of solution or product category):
that (statement of value, benefit, breakthrough capability):
unlike (reference competition or current, alternative solution):
our product/solution (does what: the key point of competitive differentiation):

BACKUP IDEA:

Table 1.3 Positioning Statement

For (clear description target customer segment):
who (have the following job to be done):
our (product/service name):
is a (type of solution or product category):
that (statement of value, benefit, breakthrough capability):
unlike (reference competition or current, alternative solution):
our product/solution (does what: the key point of competitive differentiation):

Sample positioning statements:

- For *online shopfront marketers* (target customer segment) who struggle to find return on investment in social media (problem/job to be done), Milia (name) is a web-based analytics tool that compiles and translates engagement metrics into actionable, prioritized task lists (type of solution). Unlike Google Analytics (competition), our software captures data across several search engines and social media platforms, providing customers with a reliable, comprehensive view of their business that they can act on immediately (key point of differentiation).

- For *recent college graduates* who have trouble making new friends after leaving campus, Friendline is a mobile app that connects individuals with shared tastes and social preferences to each other without awkward introductions or false starts. Unlike sports leagues and other activity-based, friend-finding solutions, our focus is on matching customers with friends who share similar interests beyond sports and drinking.

1.7   Destination: Reflection and Next Steps

Now that you have gone through idea generation, you have officially taken your first step in the entrepreneurial process. You can now move on to the next chapter or do some more tweaking—you are in control. Be cautious, however, of trying to create a perfect idea right away. As in most projects, perfectionism can become the enemy of progress. There are, however, a few useful things you can do:

- Rewrite your positioning statement a few times so that it flows well and is easy for a naïve listener (someone who has not heard the idea before and does not have any domain expertise) to understand. Try reading the statement aloud to make sure it sounds natural. Doing this may help you get rid of awkward turns of phrase that may be indicators of confused reasoning or non sequiturs.

- With a positioning statement ready, you can start exposing it to external feedback. Start with members of the founding team if you are not a solo founder. It is beneficial for each member of the founding team to complete the exercises in this chapter independently and, at a joint meeting, reconcile the different versions of ideas. Hold off on speaking with too many customers before you identify customer personae in the upcoming chapters.

- Access supplementary resources—published articles, videos, other media—that can help you consider alternative solutions, and build your toolkit by visiting the resource page on the MIT Press website (https://mitpress.mit.edu/massa-wild). Content related to this chapter can be found under Founder Resources/Chapter 1. It is important to have fun with your ideas and play with the concepts you learned in this chapter. The idea-generating process is never over. After all, entrepreneurship is a creative process that requires a commitment to flexibility and playfulness!

Finding Your First Customer

Objectives

- Describe a persona representative of the first customer segment to which you will market and sell your solution.
- Contrast potential persona profiles to ensure they are the best fit for a sensible market entry strategy.

2.1 Mini Case: Luna Finds Its Focus

When Jeanne and Stephen Luna decided to build Luna Botanicals, a business centered on their interest in plant life and green spaces, they let their passion guide them into undertaking many cool projects. The couple found themselves running planting workshops at a local food hall, taking on interior design projects for homeowners, selling plants through their website, doing event styling at weddings, and occasionally taking on larger commercial projects wherein they curated and maintained greenery for stores and restaurants. The Lunas felt very successful; they were, after all, always busy with a new project. The feedback they received was also great—people got a lot out of the workshops, residential clients were excited to share their hip spaces on social media, and commercial clients were getting great reactions from their own customers and suppliers.

Unfortunately, Jeanne and Stephen noticed that although they were busy all the time, they were not making much more profit than they were when they first started the business. They felt as though they had to scramble to get to the next project as soon as one job was complete: "We were stuck constantly hustling, not able to schedule conferences, buying trips, or the nature retreats that kept us energized and gave us ideas for new and interesting projects." It turns out that sourcing new clients, buying supplies for custom orders, and planning new and interesting workshops took not only time but significant capital. For many of the projects, expenses were either outpacing or barely exceeding revenues. Following their passion wherever it led had helped them build a solid reputation and a strong following but had not translated into the rewards they had envisioned.

Equipped with some knowledge about demand in each area they had dabbled in and a sense of which kinds of project paid off and which didn't, they began to develop a filter for what projects to take on and what projects were best left to someone else. The focal point of their attempts to make their business more profitable was a search for their core customer. The Lunas knew that the key to profitability at this relatively early stage was to find a customer that would pay well for a service they knew how to provide well. This "golden goose" was a well-resourced customer they could "wow" time and again. Such customers would become reliable evangelists for the Lunas' brand and for the integration of curated greenery into spaces. Ideally, meeting the needs of these customers would not require that the startup break the bank sourcing new suppliers and coming up with pedagogical content.

After creating profiles for each of their current customers and contrasting the pros and cons of marketing to and working with each customer type, they settled on commercial developers and designers working on commercial spaces as their core customers. By focusing on large-scale installations for these customers and meticulously targeting their marketing and sales efforts, Jeanne and Stephen could leverage the aesthetic that made them unique while making a lot more money. With careful evaluation of every opportunity and a clearer understanding of their customer base, everything felt more intentional: "We control exactly what our offerings and distribution are, and have integrated our specific offerings into our overall workflow, rather than being spread thin with many random requests." When they were not working on these big projects, they devoted resources to attracting high-paying clients: Their workshops became an invitation-only channel through which to reach developers and designers rather than a revenue source. Their website transitioned from a plant e-commerce site to a sleek portfolio for what they now referred to as their "biophilic art" installations. Their brand was now high end, but accessible via a universally appealing mission of connecting people through nature. In describing their journey to profitability, Jeanne notes that she wished she had thought systematically about what customers to target and which opportunities to avoid earlier in the venture's development: "Once we found clarity on whom we were selling to, it was so much easier to focus."

2.2 Orientation: Customer Discovery

Now that you have gone through the idea generation process, you should have a positioning statement that encapsulates your idea and conveys how you plan to frame the value of your solution. You have identified a job to be done and suggested, in broad strokes, who might need that job done. A clear and pressing job to be done is a great starting point for a discussion about a potential business, but not all people or organizations in dire need of a creative solution like yours are able to buy your solution. For instance, though graduating college students might have a pressing need for access to fresh, healthy food, they might not be able to afford the higher price tag or might not order healthy food often enough to sustain the business. Many founders find out about issues of this kind only after they have invested significant time and resources into a startup. There is, however, a better way to get to know your customer. By being empathic and stepping into your customer's shoes in a systematic way, you can gain an understanding of the needs (i.e., what they really want rather than what they say they want), characteristics (e.g., demographics, availability of funds), and behaviors (e.g., when and how they buy products and services) of your potential customer base.* Based on what you learn from trying to perceive the world through their eyes and interacting with them as deeply and as often as possible,[1] you can start taking steps to impress customers with a solution that really fits them instead of being surprised by how fast they disregard your solution.

We will now take a deep dive into who this initial customer (whether a direct consumer or a member of an organization with its own budget) in need of your solution might be. *The objective of this chapter is to help you not just avoid building a solution to fit a customer that is mildly interested in your solution but to identify a customer segment that is wholly interested in working with you to accomplish a job to be done.* Let's start by coming up with an informed, detailed best guess.

2.3 Step 1: Describing a Useful Customer Persona

A **persona** is humanized description of a customer that includes details that might not be obviously pertinent to the business but that clue one in to how they live and make buying decisions. Personae are amalgams of customers who exhibit key similarities and represent a core, likely, potential customer. They are standard tools at design and marketing firms for a good reason: when used properly, they provide a mental model of a customer that managers and employees can refer to as they make decisions about how to build and sell their products and services.[2] They can serve as a metaphor to anchor the points of view of diverse team members trying to create something amazing for a customer. While this sort of creative enterprise can lead team members in wildly divergent directions, the persona serves as the voice of the customer sitting on the shoulders of and guiding eager founders. As the Luna Botanicals case illustrates, it is easy for founders to follow their passions into what seem like equally viable and tempting business opportunities. A well-articulated persona can help keep founders focused on what matters to a customer who really needs a job to be done tackled and who is willing to pay well for it.[3]

You might have learned, either in a marketing class or an online guide, that the way you describe a customer segment is by enumerating specific demographics: "white male,

---

*Empathy is a cognitive and affective process fostering the capability of understanding and appreciating the feelings, thoughts, and experiences of others. Along with passion and perseverance, it is often considered a key competency of an entrepreneurial mindset. Russell Korte, Karl A. Smith, and Cheryl Qing Li, "The Role of Empathy in Entrepreneurship: A Core Competency of the Entrepreneurial Mindset," *Advances in Engineering Education* 7, no. 1 (2018): n1.

twenty-five to thirty-two years old, with an income over $50,000 per year." But who is this person? How would you figure out what new product or feature he might like? Listing demographics is very different from creating a persona that helps you understand a customer segment. The reality is that profiles built solely on demographics are not very discussable or testable. Age range and income are useful pieces of information, but they make up only a small piece of what is needed to craft a useful persona profile. What might a useful persona profile look like?

The first step is to go back to the positioning statement that emerged from your work on the previous chapter. Try to visualize the person you think would be most interested in have the job to be done you posed tackled right now. For whom is this an urgent, high-priority problem? Who would jump at the chance of buying a solution to this job to be done? Here is a sample positioning I showed you in the previous chapter:

> For *recent college graduates* who have trouble making new friends after leaving campus, Friendline is a mobile app that connects individuals with shared tastes and social preferences to each other without awkward introductions or false starts. Unlike local sports leagues and other activity-based, friend-finding solutions, our focus is on matching customers with friends who share similar interests beyond sports and drinking.

In this example, the customer is a college graduate who has trouble making friends after graduating and moving away. As we begin to visualize a persona that represents this customer, we might want to sketch out a profile that makes our fuzzy thoughts tangible and allows us to share them with others. I came up with Rahul as my best guess for what this potential customer might be like. Each of your team members might independently come up with different ideas of what the customer might look like. It is important that you capture and talk through these choices so that you can better understand why it is that your teammates see Roger or Tanya as better representations of your primary customer than Rahul.

The name Rahul does not give us a very good idea of what Rahul is all about, so one step a lot of entrepreneurs take is to give the customer a role. In this case, I decided that the reason Rahul had trouble making new friends after college is that he took a demanding job in a new town where he did not know anyone. When Friday night came around all he wanted to do was catch up on sleep so that he could be ready to unpack moving boxes Saturday morning. Now that we have a backstory, we can refer to our customer as **Rahul, the busy out-of-towner**. I am positing here that Rahul's situation is not unusual. I assume that many people leave the structured life of college, where friendships can be built on the shared struggles of surviving exams, and enter a world where co-workers are busy with their own families and established network of friends. Friendships, in this difficult new life chapter, must be actively maintained. Building friendships in this context is the "job to be done" the Friendline app helps Rahul tackle.

Once you come up with a viable reason for why this persona might have an interest in your solution and bake that into a brief role description, you can (1) expand the narrative by crafting a broad description of the persona's frustration or situation (a backstory),

(2) add likely demographic variables that you think might constrain your target market (e.g., age, gender, income, geographic location), and (3) capture any psychographic differences that might give you a more nuanced view of the customer. For instance, while demographics for Rahul might include age (twenty-three to thirty-six years old), income (between $28,000 and $56,000), ethnicity (Indian), marital status (single), and other relatively straightforward characteristics, psychographics measure customers' attitudes and interests rather than objective demographic criteria. Let us look at a description of buyer preferences by Alexandra Samuel that focuses on psychographics:

> Parents who trust their kids to make their own tech decisions (whom I call "enablers") tend to evaluate their tech purchases in terms of fun and entertainment value. Parents who focus on minimizing screen time ("limiters") gravitate towards software and devices that support their kids' literacy, math, and academic skills. Parents who actively guide and encourage their kids' technology use typically look for purchases that offer a balance of fun and educational value, and that offer ways to engage and play as a family.[4]

Notice that the focus of the quoted passage is on what parents think and feel rather than on their socioeconomic status or social media savvy. They capture something that is arguably as important as those details. If we turn our focus back to Rahul, we can try to come up with specific psychographics that matter for his buying behaviors. We believe it is likely that Rahul is interested in engaging in activities that will make him feel as though he is better integrated into his community and that he enjoys thinking and talking about traveling. We believe he feels lonely in the evenings after work and on the weekends. These are, of course, only unfounded hypotheses at this point, but they help humanize Rahul and provide starting points for discussion when thinking about product development and touchpoints for marketing campaigns. The persona profile in table 2.1 captures a rich picture of Rahul across various dimensions.

After drafting a persona, you will probably have a strong sense of all the things you do not know or suspect you know but have not observed. This is normal. At this stage, personae are only an honest guess at who your customer might be. In later chapters, you will do a lot of work to verify the hypotheses you have posed here and make your persona even better. Importantly, no persona is a static picture. A conscientious founder should be constantly updating and tweaking a handful of personae—usually three or four for a new venture—as the venture gets off the ground.

Action: Now that we have drafted *Rahul, the busy out-of-towner* and potential customer of Friendline, it is your turn to draft a persona from scratch. Remember to start by going back to your positioning statement and visualizing the customer who you think is your most likely first, core customer. Once you do, start working through the Persona Profile (table 2.2).

Now that you've completed one persona profile, create another that is just as compelling (table 2.3). Most businesses cannot grow by relying too heavily on a customer type for very long. Also, you might want to have a backup in case you are unable to find

Table 2.1 Persona Profile (Completed)

Customer Name	Role	
Rahul	Busy out-of-towner	
Representative Photo	**Key Demographic Details**	**Behavioral Characteristics**
	Age: 24 years Gender: Male Family: Single Education: Undergrad degree in marketing Location: Greater Miami, Fla. Income: $42,000 Job details: Customer service rep at SMB, a 148-employee, remote access software company Employment: 15 weeks in current role	• Works at office park with occasional remote work from home • Commutes 1 hour per day • Orders gourmet food delivered twice a week; likes to cook • Likes to stay on top of restaurant trends via online forums and websites • Has complete control over purchasing decisions
Representative Quote(s)		
"I had no idea I would be this busy so quickly." "I feel as though all I do is go to work and go home. I could use some social time."		
Jobs to Be Done	**Pain Points**	**Perceived Obstacles**
• Meet people whom I enjoy being around. • Make me feel that my life is not just my job.	• Social support system from college is no longer available, so Rahul is lonely and stressed.	• Lack of time to engage in discoving opportunities for socialization • Hesitant to approach strangers
Physical Hangouts	**Online Hangouts**	
• Likes to attend pop-ups and food truck rallies, indie music concerts, and to play trivia games • Goes to workplace happy hour with older colleagues • Homebody on weekday nights	• Digital native in social media; heavy exposure to chat and text messaging apps • Uses laptop in office and iPad at home; uses mobile phone to track emails, texts, and to keep up with news and Instagram; checks Facebook for family news	

Table 2.2 Persona Profile (Blank)

Customer Name	Role	
Representative Photo	Key Demographic Details	Behavioral Characteristics
Representative Quote(s)		
Jobs to Be Done	Pain Points	Perceived Obstacles
Physical Hangouts	Online Hangouts	

Table 2.3   Persona Profile (Blank)

Customer Name	Role	
Representative Photo	Key Demographic Details	Behavioral Characteristics
Representative Quote(s)		
Jobs to Be Done	Pain Points	Perceived Obstacles
Physical Hangouts	Online Hangouts	

versions of your first persona in the real world when you start conducting interviews. Remember to make the second persona distinct enough from the first persona for it to be helpful in guiding founding team discussions or formulating marketing campaigns.

You can continue to create personae if you think they are truly representative of an initial group of customers your business needs to reach to succeed. If you are in a **multisided market** (sometimes called "platforms")[†] where you are serving two or more end users at the same time, you'll have to create at least one persona for each side (e.g., one for the person buying goods on eBay and another for the person selling goods). Note, however, that a big reason for creating these profiles is to give your team focus. If too many profiles are guiding your decision-making, you might end up creating products that are agreeable to a lot of different kinds of people but wow no one. Getting those first few customers to pay attention to an upstart product or service like yours will require something truly exceptional!

2.4   Route Monitoring: Persona Reality Check

While the persona drafting exercise can be a fun way to guess what your customers might be like, it is important to make sure that your personae are informed, reasonable guesses. To make sure that your early-stage personae are viable, review them and make sure they exhibit these five characteristics:

1. **Realistic.** You should be able to coherently describe your persona in a way that allows somebody unfamiliar with your product or service to believe that person exists in the real world. That is, the characteristics, such as demographics, and your descriptors must be *believable*.

2. **Sizable.** It's usually not cost-effective to target customer segments that are too small to support even a small business. A persona, therefore, must be representative of a customer segment that is large enough to support, perhaps in combination with one or two other personae, a business in its first two years of existence.

3. **Accessible.** It sounds obvious, but your company should be able to reach its customer segments via communication and distribution channels. When it comes to hip gen-Z customers, for example, your company should have access to the latest social media and know how to use them authentically—or, in some cases, reach out to celebrities or influencers with an active social media presence to do some of your marketing for you. If you are entering the market for yacht accessories, consider whether you have the connections necessary to gain access to your ideal high-status, high-net-worth customer base.

[†]Multisided markets or platforms are distinct from traditional markets in that they enable direct interactions between two or more distinct sides. Moreover, each side is affiliated with the platform as a buyer or seller, supplier or producer, and so forth. Many of these markets are facilitated through software programs that reduce costs and friction in each transaction. David S. Evans, Andrei Hagiu, and Richard Schmalensee, *Invisible Engines: How Software Platforms Drive Innovation and Transform Industries* (Cambridge, MA: MIT Press, 2008).

Table 2.4 Persona Ranking

	Persona 1					Persona 2				
	Weak————————————Strong					Weak————————————Strong				
Realistic	1	2	3	4	5	1	2	3	4	5
Sizable	1	2	3	4	5	1	2	3	4	5
Accessible	1	2	3	4	5	1	2	3	4	5
Stable	1	2	3	4	5	1	2	3	4	5
Distinguishable	1	2	3	4	5	1	2	3	4	5
Total	Enter sum here					Enter sum here				

4. **Stable**. For a marketing campaign to be successful, a customer type should be stable enough for a long enough period to be marketed to strategically. For example, fandom is often used to segment markets (e.g., our market is Justin Bieber fans).[5] But characteristics such as preferences for artists are constantly evolving. Thus, customer segmenting based on that variable might not be wise.

5. **Distinguishable**. Your personae may have similar problems that are tackled by your solution. They must, however, also have clear distinguishing characteristics that influence their behavior, such as their ability or willingness to purchase. If they are largely similar, it is not worthwhile splitting the focus of your founding team across multiple customer types. Instead, start with a single persona and let other profiles emerge from customer interviews and early sales.

Action: Examine each of your persona profiles carefully and score them 1 (very weak) to 5 (very strong) on each characteristic.

Whichever persona came out ahead should be the first persona you try to validate exists in the real world. If no persona has a tier 1 job to be done awaiting your solution and your assumptions about them don't pan out, you can always go back to the drawing board and craft new persona profiles that are informed by your initial interviews in the field. Remember, a persona is just a hypothesis that will be revised several times before you find a business model that takes off.

2.5 Destination: Reflection and Next Steps

Personae are useful only if they are kept alive by a founding team. They must become part of day-to-day conversations. They should be easy to deploy as examples to illustrate why adopting a product feature or promotion makes sense. Here are some other uses for personae and steps you can take to make them into even more helpful representations:

- One might argue that for some ventures, such as those pushing exclusively app-based or web-based solutions, knowing the **location** of your customer is not necessarily of prime importance. I find that understanding where your customer chooses to live and why can be useful for most businesses. So, as your persona profile gains complexity, consider gaining a better understanding of not just the variables we focused on in this chapter but location-based variables. For instance, you might want to know whether your customers live in urban, suburban, or rural areas. Do they commute between home and work? Knowing this kind of information can help you decide, for instance, whether radio advertising or highway billboard advertising is at all appropriate.

- An important aspect to understand about your persona is what **other products or services** they buy regularly or are particularly excited about purchasing. After all, the part of this person's life you are trying to understand most deeply is how they find out about products or services and how they decide on a purchase. It might be helpful, therefore, to compile a short list of other brands this persona interacts with or cares about. How does your brand compare to the brands the persona is already satisfied with?

- Consult the resource page on the MIT Press website (https://mitpress.mit.edu/massa -wild). Content related to this chapter can be found under Founder Resources/Chapter 2.

3 Validating the Opportunity

Objectives

- Embed yourself into the customer community you are targeting with the help of experts.
- Put together a structured interview protocol and conduct interviews that will help you produce useful responses that propel your understanding of your customers and what job they need done.

3.1 Mini Case: Unlocking Customer Insights

After years working as a real estate agent, Barret Blondeau felt frustrated. Deals that might require two or more months of work sourcing clients, setting up open houses, putting together financing, and scheduling inspection would often fall through for what seemed to him to be trivial reasons. Others would go through as soon as a "for sale" sign went up. As the market ebbed and flowed, there were just as many periods of plenty, replete with closings, as there were periods of scarcity, during which everything seemed to fall through. Meanwhile, homeowners who trusted agents to sell their houses could not help but feel unsure of what exactly the commission they were paying agents was getting them. In short, real estate transactions were plagued with uncertainty and few win-win scenarios: "Someone always felt like they were holding the short end of the stick—the homeowner who paid 5 or 6 percent commission on a house that sold in a couple of days felt like they should have just listed the house themselves and pocketed the commission. The agent who took on a house that sat on the market for months ended up feeling like the commission didn't really match the effort they put into making the sale happen."

Barrett wanted to make the experience of buying and selling houses more transparent so that all parties could feel more in control of the process. He knew that he could not stop market slowdowns, but he thought he could make the market more efficient and tackle a real and pressing problem by creating software to guide sellers and buyers through real estate transactions. He hoped he could do what companies like Intuit (maker of TurboTax) did for professionals frustrated by the onerous process of filling out tax forms. Barrett's hypothesis for a job to be done was getting less and less fuzzy and the basic concept for Falaya was materializing. So he took the next step and, together with his founding team, brainstormed potential customers who might be willing to experiment with a new way of doing things. Who might these initial customers be?

Barrett could have relied on years of professional experience to make an educated guess as to whom he should market Falaya to first. But instead of assuming he already had a complete picture of his market, he began having conversations with other agents at first, and then with buyers and sellers. He used those informal conversations to craft a set of questions that he thought would tell him whether people would be legitimately interested in using Falaya but did not tell them much about the software itself. After all, he did not want these potential customers to feel as though he was just trying to push his own idea of what they needed down their throat. His questions tended to be open-ended. He enjoyed prompting people to tell him horror stories of real estate transactions gone wrong or amazing experiences they would like to have again. After his interviews numbered in the dozens, he started noticing that he was getting similar responses again and again. It seemed that each interview was leading to less and less surprising information. So he took a break from sourcing new interviews and started reflecting on what he had discovered.

He found that first-time homebuyers and people uncomfortable with using software-based solutions like Falaya were unlikely to be willing to go through an entire transaction without the support of a dedicated agent. That did not mean they would not use Falaya eventually, only that he would need to build a network of trained agents whom buyers could reach out to for help if anything went wrong before he began marketing to them. The same was true of people who were not price-sensitive enough to feel an urgent need to make 5 percent more money on a transaction. After all, they just wanted to have the worries and labor taken completely out of their hands. The people who seemed most excited about tackling the problems Barrett posed were people who already understood the ins and outs of real estate transactions. These were experienced (i.e., serial) home sellers marketing houses in hot neighborhoods and experienced buyers who had already gone through the process several times before. Contractors and developers selling houses they had built themselves, investors flipping houses, and professionals who moved frequently stood out because of their enthusiasm during interviews. It was time to start thinking about building a prototype that would wow these customers.

3.2   Orientation: Opportunity Validation

Perhaps the most prevalent and damaging myth aspiring entrepreneurs ascribe to is that of the lone genius in the garage.[1] The narrative goes something like this: the nerdy loner, struck suddenly with a wonderful idea, retires to a garage somewhere in Silicon Valley and builds the next big thing. Inspiring and pervasive as it may be, this myth gets it wrong in many ways, chiefly in the notion that the building blocks of a successful startup—ideas, business models, prototypes—emerge out of the hard work of an isolated genius. Entrepreneurship is and has mostly been a social phenomenon.[2] Successful entrepreneurs tend to spend more time talking to others about their ideas and refining them via feedback than they do sitting around thinking about clever ways to solve problems. By and large, nascent, unrefined, and untested ideas have little intrinsic value, so hoarding ideas until they are ready for market makes little sense.

Sadly, even entrepreneurs who ignore the myths and decide to go through cycles of feedback tend to work hard to get others to confirm the views they already have.[*] After all, talking to strangers and asking them to be critical of an idea you are likely passionate about is nobody's idea of fun. It is, nevertheless, a critical step in the process of making an idea market ready. To succeed in a competitive market, you must challenge your preconceptions about what job you are helping a customer to accomplish before these preconceptions challenge you. This means you must actively seek out the highest-quality evidence possible to support or counter the hypotheses that underlie your nascent business idea.

This chapter guides you through the key steps you need to take to gather evidence that the opportunity you are pursuing is worthwhile before you spend your life savings and time on it. It begins by tackling the first two elements of an opportunity that require external validation:

1. The job to be done you are tackling (i.e., what potential customers are trying to get done) not only exists but is both pervasive and pressing. That is, enough people to sustain an early-stage startup have this problem and it is urgent enough that they will be clamoring to pay for a solution.

2. The persona you hypothesized needs this job handled is the right beachhead customer. That is, the persona is part of a customer segment that really wants to tackle the job to be done at hand (i.e., your target is truly unsatisfied with the status quo), is willing to pay for it, and is actively seeking a solution. Can you sell to someone who does not fit all these criteria? Possibly. But remember, your goal here is to identify the initial, core customer segment that is going to really be wowed by your solution.

In 1960, Professor Theodore Levitt coined the term **marketing myopia** to describe the blunder of defining a business by product features or industry rather than by what the business actually accomplished for customers; he noted that the railroad companies were in dire financial trouble not because the need for passenger and freight transportation declined or was better met by substitutes (cars, trucks, airplanes) but because the managers of railroad companies were railroad-oriented rather than transportation-oriented. They were product-oriented instead of customer-oriented and could not see creative solutions outside their own domain.[†]

---

[*]Confirmation bias (alternatively known as confirmatory or my-side bias) is a tendency to search for or interpret information in a way that confirms one's preconceptions. One might, for instance, cherry-pick pieces of information gleaned from customer interactions that support one's own views of how a market operates rather than dig for evidence that might challenge existing beliefs.

[†]Theodore Levitt, "Marketing Myopia," *Harvard Business Review* 3, no. 4 (July/August 1960): 45–56; reprinted in *Harvard Business Review* 53, no. 5 (September/October 1975).

Crucially, your goal at this point should not be to engage in solution validation or to get lots of customer feedback on features. In fact, it is imperative that you *do not share your ideas for a solution with potential customers* until you understand your customer persona and the job to be done thoroughly. Instead, you should focus on profiling your initial customers and the jobs they are concerned with tackling and not on the color, shape, or size of your product. The Falaya team was careful not to talk about or refer to their prototype or other solution ideas that were available to them while conducting their interviews. Instead, they listened intently. Their focus was on what real estate agents, homeowners, and home buyers were experiencing as pain points in their real estate transaction and what imperfect, alternative solutions they were deploying to mitigate these pain points. After all, customers want to know that you are building a solution to their problems and that you are listening to their insights instead of trying to push your own. If you validate the solution without validating the hypothesis that the job to be done matches the needs of your initial persona, you will end up building a shiny product or service no one really wants or needs. Do not follow in the myopic footsteps of the American railroad industry highlighted in the box.[3] Remember, this first wave of interviews represents a great chance for you to learn about the customers that will make or break your startup, and not your chance to make a sale!

3.3   Step 1: Embedding in Communities and Discovering Experts

Identifying an initial list of contacts can be an onerous task for someone who is not already part of an industry. That is why people who have worked in, analyzed, or served an industry tend to have a better idea how to sell solutions in the same domain.[4] The founding team's experience enhances both new venture survival and sales.[5] The team knows the "lay of the land," including who the decision-makers are, what the sales cycle looks like, what obstacles exist, and where resources helpful to jump-starting a business can be found. If you are not an insider, a good starting point is to try to identify industry experts or people with deep experience to explain how things work. These **experts** often know other people who might also serve as good interview subjects and might refer you to them if you make a good impression (serial referrals are known as the "snowball" sampling technique). In addition to a couple of domain experts, you will also want to find interview subjects who are a good fit for the personae you identified earlier. These should make up the bulk of your early-stage interviews.

It is also important to begin identifying clusters of potential customers that make up the **community** you plan to serve. Word of mouth typically travels via communities, either online[6] or offline, for people are more likely to intimately know the needs of others they interact with regularly. They are also more likely to discuss products and services during these regular interactions,[7] generating "buzz."[8] Consider your own case: Who was the last person to recommend a product or service to you? Why did that person share what they knew, and how did they share it? Knowing the underlying social dynamics behind word-of-mouth diffusion of information is crucial to a new business that cannot invest much in marketing. One way to do this is to embed yourself in the community by attending industry and networking events open to outsiders. Consider also where you choose to work every day. Will being in a coworking space or a coffee shop increase your exposure to your customers or potential experts? If so, consider structuring your day to maximize the likelihood of serendipitous interactions.

Action: First, list eight potential interviewees that are good matches for your persona (table 3.1). Rate these people on a scale of 1 to 5, based on how well they fit your hypothesized persona and how urgent you believe solving the problem or job to be done will be for them. Once you are satisfied with your persona list, select two people who qualify as experts and who you believe might help you gain access to the people you listed, or who might help you improve the quality of the persona list. If you can't find two or three people who might fit your persona hypothesis, you might want to go back to the drawing board and come up with a product or service that is compelling to more people. It is important not to be afraid of asking people you think might be customers for introductions to people *they* think might be potential customers, and so on.

Table 3.1 Interviewee List

Customer Name	Job Title, Relevant Role, Employer	Email, Phone	Rate 1 (very low) to 5 (very high)	
			Fit with Persona	Urgency of Job to Be Done
1				
2				
3				
4				
5				
6				
7				
8				
9				
10				
Expert Name	Job Title, Relevant Role, Employer	Email, Phone	Qualifications as Expert	
1				
2				

With this list in place, you can begin to consider how to convince these people to sit down with you for a face-to-face interview (or a remote interview by video if an in-person meeting is not possible). In my experience, successful requests for an interview tend to focus not on you or the success of your business but on the interviewee. They also depend on your eagerness to better understand the kinds of problems interviewees face or to absorb some of their hard-earned expertise. As usual, a well-crafted email with no typos or overly "salesy" language is more likely to yield results. Couple that with a well-timed follow-up phone call, and you might just get what you want.

Next, look online for events, meetups, conferences, or any other social occasions where you might find additional interview subjects. List any you find in table 3.2.

3.4   Step 2: Creating an Interview Protocol

A great opportunity validation interview is typically not something you will get on your first attempt. Professional reporters and researchers spend years honing their interview skills and checking their own biases so that the information they gather is not tainted. They strive to adopt a mindset that is guided by curiosity and empathy rather than the mindset of an inquisitor seeking answers they already believe to be true.[‡] They make sure they are respectful of their interviewee's time and dignity because they know that the easiest way to get an interview cut short is to ask questions that don't seem well thought out or that offend the person sitting across from them. Practicing conducting interviews with the right mindset will help make you a more effective data gatherer.

That does not mean, however, that inexperienced interviewers cannot gather useful data. By having access to a set of structured questions that are well crafted, the interviewer will fumble less and spend less time thinking about what to ask next. A structured set of questions is also useful because it allows:

- different teammates to ask the same questions and compare results after the fact;
- the interviewer to experiment with changing the question order or tweaking questions and observing what changes in responses ensue; and
- forgoing asking questions that keep getting very similar response after a while (otherwise known as data saturation).[§]

[‡] In his famous book, *The Ethnographic Interview* (Belmont, CA: Waveland Press, 2016; first published in 1979) and reissued multiple times since then), James P. Spradley captures the mindset of a scholar seeking to understand their interview subject and not to simply verify their own ideas. He writes: "I want to understand the world from your point of view. I want to know what you know in the way you know it. I want to understand the meaning of your experience, to walk in your shoes, to feel things as you feel them, to explain things as you explain them. Will you become my teacher and help me understand?" (34).

[§] Data saturation refers to the point in the research process when no new information is discovered in data analysis, and this redundancy signals to researchers that data collection may cease. Saturation means that a researcher can be reasonably assured that further data collection would yield similar results and serve to confirm emerging themes and conclusions. See Sandra L. Faulkner and Stormy P. Trotter, "Data Saturation,"

Table 3.2 Event List

	Event Name	Planned Date(s)	Why is this event appropriate for job or persona discovery?
1			
2			
3			
4			
5			
6			
7			
8			
9			
10			

This does not mean, of course, that you should read out questions like an automaton and record results without adapting to what the person has said. To do so would impair what makes interviews a better exploratory gathering tool than an online survey: the opportunity for unexpected insight.

So, when you are asking questions and your subject answers the question in an interesting way, don't be afraid to ask them to elaborate or clarify, or to ask follow-up questions that might yield something meaningful.

It is also important to note that you probably will not be able to gather all the information you need to validate that someone fits your persona and job to be done hypothesis in a single interview. In fact, it is more likely that an initial interview might serve to validate that a customer should be part of your sample by giving you a sense of who they are and how they are experiencing the problem your solution purports to solve. It is only once you have validated that the problem is real and urgent to a potential customer and you've captured how they are currently solving the problem that you should even mention your amazing solution (in a separate interview, after you have had time to digest their relationship with the job to be done). I'll repeat it because this is a key tenet of the lean startup philosophy: don't try to describe your solution (much less sell it) before you

in *The International Encyclopedia of Communication Research Methods*, ed. Jörg Matthes (Hoboken, NJ: John Wiley & Sons, 2017): 1–2.

Table 3.3 Sample Opportunity Validation Questions

Category	Instructions	Sample Questions
Persona Validation	Depending on how you obtained the interview or how much background you have on the person, you may need to make sure they fit your chosen beachhead, or learn more about their demographics or psychographics.	• Tell me more about your role in your currently job/ household. • Who handles [job-to-be-done domain] in your home/office? Why? • How much time do you spend on [job-to-be-done-related activities]? Does that seem like a lot? • [Specific questions related to your customer's daily life—for example:] Do you have kids? How do you make buying decisions? Do you have hobbies?
Job-to-Be-Done Discovery	These questions are designed to help you figure what tier 1 problems your interviewee might have. Do not "lead the witness" by asking specifically about problems, and note that all questions are open-ended.	• What is the hardest part of your day? • What are some unmet needs or annoying issues you have in your job/in your household/when you go out? • What tasks take up the most time in your day? • What could be done to improve your experience with [process/role]? • What is the hardest part about being in your [demographic/role/job]? • What are your biggest/most important professional/personal responsibilities/goals?
Job-to-Be-Done Validation	If your customer did not talk about the problem you wanted to address with the previous set of questions, use this set to begin validating or invalidating that your customer has the problem you think they have.	• Do you find it hard to do [job to be done]? • How important is [value you are delivering] to you? • Tell me about the last time you [did the job-related activity you are tackling]. (Listen for complaints.) • Do you currently try to tackle [job to be done] in any way? (Listen for alternative solutions.) • How motivated are you to solve/improve [the problem/process]? • If you had a solution to this problem, what would it mean to you/how would it affect you?
Ending the Initial Interview	It is important to get the interviewee to validate your interpretation of what they have told you. This is also your opportunity to ask for new interview referrals or to open the door to yourr asking more questions in the future.	• (Summarize key takeaways): Is that accurate? • So, based on the conversation, it sounds like *x* is really hard/very important to you, but *y* is not. How accurate is that? • Is there anything else you think I should know about that I did not ask? • Do you know anyone else who might also have this problem that I could ask similar questions of? (It is a small form of validation if they are willing to give you referrals.) • May I keep **you** in the **loop on how the product** develops? May I reach out once I put together a mockup/prototype? • May I follow up with you if I have more questions?

have validated that the person has an urgent problem on their hands that you might be able to tackle.

This means that you should ask mostly open-ended questions (those that lead to long responses, such as stories) rather than closed-ended ones (those that lead to much less useful yes-or-no responses). After all, if what you are interested in is yes-or-no responses, a survey can do the job and cost you a lot less time.

Typical opportunity validation interviews tend to focus on saturating broad categories that, unsurprisingly, are catchalls for questions that have the potential either to validating or invalidate assumptions. Table 3.3 lays out an abridged sampling of potentially relevant persona and job-to-be-done validation questions. It goes without saying that many of these questions may be fitting or not, depending on the kind of venture you are starting. Use them as a starting point and customize as needed. Make your interview protocol fit what you need to know and what you are curious about!

Action: Now it is your turn to try your hand at building your own opportunity validation interview protocol, using the protocol blank in table 3.4. Consider the first or second most promising person on your contact list. What kinds of questions do you need to ask them? How much time can they afford to give you? Make sure you leave at least three to five minutes for each response, and have some follow-up questions ready in case the person you are speaking with ends up giving you short answers. *Remember to get a sense of what the job to be done is and how important it is to this person, and to start with open-ended questions that elicit rich stories.*

Once you have completed your interview protocol form, rehearse the interview questions at least once with a friend. You may find that some questions do not sound quite right or that you are not getting the quality of responses you were expecting, so go back to the drawing board. Also, your protocol should change depending on how far along your business has come and your sense of how much evidence you have collected to support the hypotheses that underlie that business.

In his explanation of early-stage customer development, Steve Blank paints a picture of the type of customer that should be your initial, lead user—the core persona in our method. He suggests that the customer should fit most, if not all, of following characteristics: (1) the potential customer has a problem, (2) they understand they have a problem, (3) they are actively searching for a solution, (4) they have cobbled together an interim, often home-grown solution, and (5) they have or can acquire a budget to purchase a better solution. Blank says, "These people are . . . the ones [to] rely on for feedback and for your first sales; the ones who will tell others about your product and spread the word."[9]

3.5   Step 3: Capturing Interview Results

Capturing interview results can be challenging. A few issues can make the process more complicated than it needs to be. They include:

Table 3.4 Interview Protocol (Blank)

1
2
3
4
5
6
7
8
9
10

- You did not record or take notes during the interview, making it nearly impossible for you to remember key details.
- Several interviewers with different ideas about how to conduct the interviews split the work of conducting interviews, creating irreconcilable data.
- The sample you selected does not match the persona you hypothesized, making it likely that the interviewee's idea of how pressing or important a problem is will be different.
- The questions you asked were not well crafted to lead to rich, open-ended responses, leaving you with data that do not really tell you more than an online survey might.

These issues surface often, even for experienced interviewers. The key to a successful interview is to get feedback not only on your ideas but on all the instruments used to collect data.[10]

Action: To help you organize and understand the results of your interviews, fill out the log in table 3.5 after each interview. It is also helpful to listen to a recording of the interview (obtained with the interviewee's permission) while you fill out the form. Begin by listing the name of the interviewee, how long the interview took, and whether you received permission to contact them again. Follow with lessons learned from the interview, an insightful quote, and any referrals received for additional interviews with other people who either are experts or fit the persona profile.

    This form should not be the only repository of data you maintain. It is meant to be shorthand and is designed as a way for you to communicate your findings with advisers

Table 3.5 Interview Log

	Interviewee Name / Date, Time Spent / Reengage?	Lessons Learned	Referral(s)
1	Name: Date: Time Spent: Permission to Reengage (Yes/No)		
2			
3			
4			

or members of your founding team. Although I only include four slots in the book, you should not restrict yourself to conducting only four interviews. In fact, you should keep going until you feel confident that all the questions posed in your protocol have been answered in the same way by several subjects. Some teams generate these worksheets and start categorizing their interviewees into persona categories, sometimes finding new and interesting potential markets in the process.

3.6   Destination: Reflection and Next Steps

Continued interaction with experts and potential customers is key to determining the best possible fit between your hypothesized persona and the job to be done. Many founders continue scheduling and conducting interviews well into investment rounds to try to keep pace with changing customer preferences and trends. Your agility as a founder and your ability to pivot your startup to react to changes in customer behavior are among the key advantages you have over more established and better-resourced players. Here are a few practices that will help you make use of those advantages:

- As you continue to learn about your persona, adapt your interview protocol by adding questions related to ongoing dilemmas and removing questions that have become saturated with repeated responses. That is, if you get the same response to a question repeatedly from different customers, asking a different question may be a better use of your time.

- Keep tabs on what interviews lead to changes in the way you formulate your hypotheses. Make note of quotes that might be illustrative for investor meetings or internal meetings. In short, keep great notes, and use the data you are gathering to inform decision-making. By making data-based decision-making a habit and taking good notes, you will likely influence the habits of your entire team.

- Consult the resource page on the MIT Press website (https://mitpress.mit.edu/massa-wild). Content related to this chapter can be found under Founder Resources/Chapter 3.

4   Designing Customer Journeys

Objectives

- Determine what your customer persona thinks, feels, and does across all phases of the customer journey map.
- Identify appropriate channels through which to reach and compel your customer persona as they undertake their journey.
- Illustrate a captivating use case through which external audiences can better understand how your solution delivers value.

4.1   Mini Case: Charming Customers

After a class in entomology at North Carolina State University (NCSU), James Boicourt was hooked on bees. His interest would drive him to take several beekeeping classes—including a few at the graduate level. He was fascinated by the bees themselves and their orderly honey production process. Between beekeeping courses, James and his friends also conducted a lot of home brewing experiments. It was only a matter of time before he combined his passions and started experimenting with mead—an alcoholic drink made of fermented honey and water. A few years, a few hundred experimental batches, and many taste tests later, James felt he had perfected his formula. Unlike other cloyingly sweet meads available at the time, the dry and refined varieties he was making were, according to his customer interviews, drinkable enough to be considered an alternative to top-rated ciders and craft beers.

After graduation, James moved to Baltimore and began laying the groundwork for Charm City Meadworks. He and partner Andrew Geffken knew that, unlike the craft breweries that had sprouted up in the area, they would have to do a lot of work to educate customers about mead: "Our biggest push is to show people that mead can be an exciting stand-alone drink." The cofounders started making mead in a single garage bay with a kegerator and a few picnic tables loaded with carboys. Their most important job, however, was having conversations with drinkers, retailers, and wholesalers. Instead of hiring someone to sell the product and learn how to sell mead for them, James and Andrew came to see the value in doing the early legwork themselves: "It allowed us to understand not only how people received our product but how we should tailor our messaging. We were new to the industry, new to working with these customers, and selling a new product—this time was unbelievably valuable."

To sell these people on the idea of mead, James and Andrew had to think very carefully about how they would frame the product. They came to realize that while the novelty of the product might get adventurous customers to try it, many people were hesitant to buy it because they saw the product as sweet and undrinkable, particularly in larger quantities. Over several meetings, the founding team members considered how they might approach the customer with intention, thinking strategically about when and how they could expose drinkers and retailers to their product. They identified key channels through which customers became aware of the existence of their product, how they evaluated beverage choices, how they preferred to purchase the product, how they actually drank the product, and finally, how they shared mead with their friends.

By approaching this "customer journey" systematically, the founding team was able to design a marketing campaign that connected with customers in the right place and at the right time. Instead of wasting time with outreach that did not appeal to their customer persona, they were engaging in targeted outreach at farmer's markets, through trivia nights, and at local events, all of which built a community of mead fans around their business. Instead of simply dropping off cans of mead at local bars, the team educated bartenders about mead and its value as a drinkable, stand-alone product or as a versatile addition to cocktails. Eventually Charm City Meadworks built its own production facility and tasting room. To keep the lineup of products fresh, the team experimented constantly with new flavors, some offered exclusively to loyal customers who visited the board game–filled tasting room. Through enlightened trial and error, by understanding customers, and by building community, Meadworks found itself barely keeping up with the buzz that now surrounded the startup's events and innovative products.

4.2 Orientation: Journey Mapping

By engaging in *opportunity validation,* you got a good sense of the daily routines of your potential customers, what problems arose as they worked and played, and perhaps even what solutions might best address their most pressing jobs to be done. *This chapter pushes you to think very carefully about* how *your customers engage with your business.* A sustainably successful business must not only address a pressing job to be done but wow customers across all steps of their experience. To accomplish this, you should not only create a great product prototype or provide stellar service but understand what we will refer to from now on as the **customer journey**. This journey typically starts when the customer, after identifying a job to be done, seeks a solution (discovery phase) and ends when the very satisfied customer is enthusiastically praising your solution to others (sharing phase). Depending on the kind of product or service you are offering and the customer persona interacting with your business, the journey may differ in scope and depth across its steps. The big takeaway, however, is that *a great product or service is not, on its own, a great business*. A great business requires careful engineering of all the steps that precede and follow the purchase and use of a solution. As the Charm City Meadworks case illustrates, coming up with a product that tasted great was only the beginning of the entrepreneurial process.

To capture the ins and outs of your customer's journey, we will be using a design thinking tool called the **customer journey map**. The journey map is used to chart the thoughts, feelings, and actions of customers (e.g., avid movie watchers) as they undergo an experience (e.g., attending a movie premier). **Design thinking** refers to a method developed by customer experience designers that, at its best, allows for businesses to empathically meet people's needs and desires.* In building the journey map, you will be stepping into your customer's shoes to try to understand your solution from their perspective. Founders can use this tool not only to map ongoing experiences but also to *imagine* what the experience of discovering, using, and sharing a hypothesized solution to a job to be done might be like for new personae.

4.3   Step 1: Laying Out and Bounding the Map

The first step of the mapping process involves (1) selecting the persona that will go through the experience and (2) bounding the experience that will be mapped. You have already picked out a persona in chapter 3. The narrower your definition of that persona, the fewer deviations from a single customer journey there will be. Also, the more information you got from your customer interviews when validating your opportunity, the more basis you will have for making good mapping decisions. Thus, this exercise should help you find out if you did thorough work when completing the preceding chapters. Note that if you are working on building a business in a multisided market, you should create a journey map for each persona needed to make the business work. Doing so will ensure that you make do not make the experience lopsided—that is, worthwhile for one side of the market and lackluster for the other.

We can bound the experience by delimiting the phases in your customer's journey. Each phase should be distinct from the others and include specific actions that separate it from the phases that precede and follow it. As the figure 4.1 illustrates, a generic

---

*According to the product design firm IDEO, design thinking has three essential pillars: (1) empathy, or understanding the needs of those you're designing for by stepping into their perspective; (2) ideation, or generating ideas in a purposeful and often systematic way through techniques such as brainstorming, triggered brainwalking, sketching, and so on; and (3) experimentation, or testing ideas using the scientific method and hands-on prototyping. These pillars align well with the basic tenets of the lean startup methodology, agile engineering, the jobs-to-be-done framework, and other theoretical and practical orientations that underlie this book. See Thomas Kelley, *The Ten Faces of Innovation: IDEO's Strategies for Beating the Devil's Advocate & Driving Creativity throughout Your Organization* (New York: Crown Business, 2005).

FIGURE 4.1
Phases of Customer Journey.

engagement experience might include the following discrete steps: (1) discover, (2) research, (3) purchase, (4) use, and (5) share.[†] Note that I define each phase by an action taken by the customer and not by actions taken by the startup's representative. After all, we are trying to map the journey from the perspective of the customer. To make sure each step is useful, they must all be clearly circumscribed. For instance, discovery includes only the period from the time a customer experiences a problem or identifies a job to be done to the time the customer becomes aware of a solution. The research phase describes the period when a customer, already aware of the existence of the solution, explores alternatives and considers the pros and cons of adoption. Purchase usually describes a point-of-sale experience or the checkout process on a website. The use phase describes the way the customer engages with or enjoys the product or service, and the sharing phase tackles how a customer might engage in advocacy of the product with friends, family, and social media contacts.

With the phases in place, we can start to consider what aspects might be useful to track across these phases. One option is to rely on a think-feel-do framework (table 4.1) to capture the customer experience in a holistic way that accounts for cognitive (thinking), affective (feeling), and behavioral (doing) aspects of the journey.[1] The content used to populate this tool should be drawn from your interviews with potential customers in your target market. Although the map is meant to capture a hypothetical journey, you need to know enough about your primary customer persona to visualize how they might interact with the business across different phases.

As table 4.1 illustrates, the **Think** row should capture analytical thoughts going through the customer's mind as they experience each phase. For instance, you might hypothesize during the research phase that the customer thinks the price of the product is high compared to the price of alternatives. The customer might also think that sharing the fact that they are using the product on social media could reflect well on them during the sharing phase. These thoughts are often represented as sentences in quotations, like thought bubbles in a comic book. The **Feel** row should capture the customer's emotional state as they interact with the business across the different phases. A customer who has a hard time finding out how to pay for a product on a badly designed website might feel frustrated and abandon the journey. The same frustration might emerge during the use

---

[†] It is important to note that many design thinking experts would balk at having predetermined steps on the journey. They would instead favor a more grounded approach whereby your deep engagement with your chosen context and customer would allow you to define steps that are as close to your customer's experience as possible. While I am not against this practice, I find it helpful to give first-time journey mappers a few guideposts that help them understand the practice.

Table 4.1 Think-Feel-Do Example

	Discover	Research	Purchase	Use	Share
Think	"If I find a solution soon, I can carve out more time for my family."	"What is the difference between product B and product C? Where is the information?"	"If I spend this much money on a solution, I won't have much left for the holiday."	"Using this software, it takes me a lot less time than it used to."	"I'm sure Sharon would appreciate this too."
Feel	*Excited* about the possibility of finding a great solution	*Confused* by the variety of options	*Troubled* that the price was not clear from the onset	*Impressed* by the design quality and ease of use	*Delighted* about how easy it was to share your thoughts with one click
Do	(1) Google keywords. (2) Email best friend.	(3) Review user comments. (4) Look for third-party reviews on a specialty website.	(5) Fill out account information. (6) Review order.	(7) Transfer information into new system. (8) Conduct analysis.	(9) Write brief testimonial in text box. (10) Share comments on social media.

phase because of product design issues. More positive emotional states such as excitement or curiosity might propel the customer through the journey and are just as important as their negative counterparts. Finally, the **Do** row describes the actions customers take or behaviors they exhibit during each phase. During the research phase, a user might, for example, engage in the following actions: (1) review user comments, (2) look for third-party reviews on a specialty website, and (3) ask expert friends for advice on which product would best serve their needs.

While table 4.1 is a simple way to display one customer's experience, more graphical versions (like the one shown in figure 4.2, which captures emotional highs and lows) can be useful when sharing customer journeys with stakeholders.

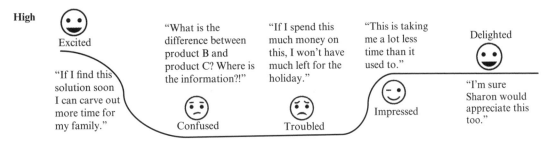

FIGURE 4.2

Illustration of Customer Journey.

Table 4.2 Think-Feel-Do (Blank)

	Discover	Research	Purchase	Use	Share
Think					
Feel					
Do					

Action: Complete your own version of the customer journey for your primary customer persona using the think-feel-do framework in table 4.2. Remember that while you should draw as much as possible from your interviews, it is likely you will have gaps in your knowledge of your customer's experience. Fill in those gaps with best guesses for now and make a note to add questions that might fill in the gaps to your interview protocol.

4.4 Step 2: Identifying Customer Touchpoints

By mapping a journey for your primary customer persona, you have taken an important first step in understanding how they might interact with your business over one engagement cycle. To best understand how you and your team can influence this journey, you will need to understand the channels through which customers are reached through their journey. These are called **touchpoints**.[2] An easy way to hypothesize what channels should be used as touchpoints across phases is to lay out the phases of the journey and see how each channel moves the customer to the next phase of engagement.

In table 4.3, you will see that different phases require engagement across different channels (e.g., social media, a landing page, or website, email newsletters, and even more traditional print media). Note that print media (e.g., a press release sent to newspapers) is hypothesized as important in the discovery phase, but not in any subsequent phases. This means that the startup in question can devote time and resources to this channel at first but reallocate resources to other channels soon thereafter. Also, for this business,

Table 4.3 Sales and Marketing Channel Usage

	Discover	Research	Purchase	Use	Share
Social Media	Conduct a targeted awareness campaign on Facebook.	Share blog articles and media product comparisons on Twitter, Facebook.	Provide links to online storefront on social media sites.	n/a	Use funny videos to encourage organic sharing on social media.
Website/Landing Page	SEO Search Engine Optimization) on Google and Bing for landing page using core key words.	Present testimonials and a table comparing solution to alternatives.	Provide easy log in and access to various payment methods.	Make how-to video and provide step-by-step guide on website.	Link to social media to share news of purchase or renewal.
Email/Newsletter	Send email to industry mailing lists with link to website.	Collect and send testimonials from industry luminaries.	Provide links to online storefront/email link-throughs.	Send email asking whether support is needed and thanking for continued patronage.	n/a
Print Media	Write press releases about company milestones with product description and value proposition.	Invite reporters to visit HQ and profile company leaders/innovators.	n/a	n/a	n/a

social media and the website act in tandem to supply information as customers research alternatives and begin to consider a purchase. It is often the case that there is some overlap between channels to reinforce a particularly vital message.

Action: Using insights from your interviews wherever possible, select and write down in table 4.4 channels that will help you push and pull customers through the journey. Try to keep in mind that different businesses will need to use different channels at different times.

4.5   Step 3: Zooming In to a Use Case

While the holistic view of the journey map is useful to help one understand where to invest time and resources, investors and early adopters often want to see the product or service in action. That is, they want to observe a demonstration of a prototype of a product or service that will give them a better idea of what the nuts and bolts of what you are proposing look like from the customer's perspective. Put differently, they want to take a "deep dive" into or "zoom in" to the use phase of the journey map to see how the job to

Table 4.4 Sales and Marketing Channel Usage (Blank)

	Discover	Research	Purchase	Use	Share
Social Media					
Website/ Landing Page					
Email/ Newsletter					
Print Media					

be done is tackled in real time (figure 4.3). This list of actions or event steps that defines the interactions between a persona and a solution (the "**use case**"[3]) usually begins when a customer walks through the doors of your store, downloads your app, reaches your website, or receives the package containing your product. As such, it cannot be richly described in a comprehensive journey map.

For instance, to illustrate the use case for an app, founders and their teams create what is referred to in the tech industry as a "demo." The demo can be "live," in which a working prototype of the app is shown, or it can be a prepackaged series of slides showing screenshots of the app or a prerecorded video. If the demo is not live, founders might use one of many available wireframing tools to create a mock version of a select number of screens in their app. A mockup for the Venmo peer-to-peer payment app might have included sequential screenshots that captured one user requesting money for a pizza party after work and the recipient of the request seamlessly transferring funds through the app interface. In a more analog case, such as a new meadery, the use case might be a series of photos on a layout of the facilities that describe all the interactions staff

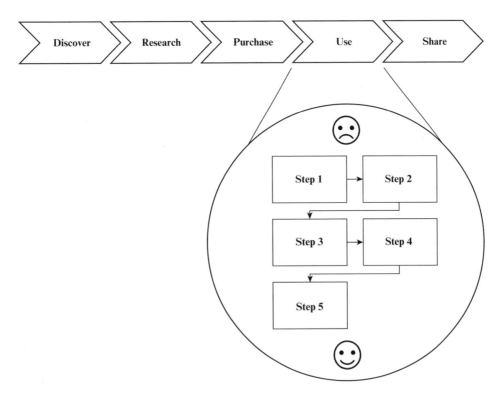

FIGURE 4.3
Zoom In to a Use Case.

might have with a new patron. In either use case, the goal is to help individuals who are not familiar with your product or service visualize the delivery of value to customers in action. In the case of the meadery, the demo can also be a useful training tool when onboarding new employees.

In short, by wrapping a compelling customer use story around images, the founders can present an instance of a customer using a solution to tackle a job to be done. The star of the story is usually the persona. The story is told from this star's perspective. It is up to you as a founder to identify the best way to demonstrate a solution to others and how much of the use case to display. Most demos remain a work in progress, being constantly revised as one interacts with different stakeholders.

Action: Create a visual demo or use case of your solution using whatever media you deem appropriate. Do not try to capture every single step in your product or service use case. Instead, focus on the highlights that would allow you to convey how to deliver value in a presentation to investors.

4.6 Destination: Reflection and Next Steps

Creating a comprehensive journey map that details all your interactions with a customer persona and a use case for your solution is only the beginning of a process that should be kept alive as you develop your startup. That is, a journey map, much like other tools discussed in this book, should never be static. Your customers' preferences, the circumstances they find themselves in, and the relevance and prioritization of jobs to be done all fluctuate over time. It is your job as an engaged entrepreneur to keep up with these changes as best you can before and after launch. There are a few steps you can take to help you do that:

- After you set up a journey map, try to make it visible to yourself and your team in a shared space (e.g., in the form of sticky notes in an office wall or as an erasable marker drawing on a white board). Encourage members of a founding team to challenge what constitutes each phase of the journey or to suggest new or different channels through which customers might be reached. By doing so, you are keeping the journey maps alive and having an ongoing conversation with teammates about how your approach to customer service is shaped.

- As your sales footprint grows and you engage with more than one persona, new journey maps will be created. Overlaying one depiction of a journey over another will yield instances (i.e., certain steps in the journey) where your efforts to interact with personae will overlap perfectly. In other cases, different personae will require you to utilize different channels or to leverage the same channel in a distinct way. This often means additional costs are aggregating because you are serving different personas in different ways. Are the costs you are adding to the journey worth the additional sales gained from the targeting of a new customer segment? If not, return to the original journey and select a different persona to target—perhaps one with greater overlap or greater yield in additional sales gained for deviations in the customer journey.

- Journey maps are useful tools to help you understand your customers, but they are also useful in helping you, as a founder and CEO, to understand the internal dynamics of *your* journey. As your team becomes more familiar with journey mapping as a tool, ask them to map their own journeys so that they can understand how to identify efficiencies and larger-scale improvements in how they work.

- Consult the resource page on the MIT Press website (https://mitpress.mit.edu/massa -wild). Content related to this chapter can be found under Founder Resources/Chapter 4.

5 Modeling Your Business

Objectives

- Design a business model that ensures customers not only see value in your solution but can be reached through channels that enhance desirability.
- Describe the activities, resources, and partners that will help you ensure the consistent delivery of your value propositions to your customer segment.
- Capture the cost structure and revenue streams that will make your business model viable in the long run.

5.1 Mini Case: Making Creative Reuse Financially Sustainable

In 1998, a group of teachers who wanted to find a home for their leftover classroom materials decided to bring all they had to A Teacher's Space, a resource center for teachers in Portland Public Schools. Typically, they would just drop off materials on a table for others to use. After noticing interest not only from teachers but also from parents and resourceful people interested in costumes, holiday decorations, and other special event crafting, a teacher named Joan Grimm sat with a few of her peers and began work on a grant application to the Department of Environmental Quality. Their goal: to open a small creative reuse center for the community. SCRAP became a 501(c)(3) nonprofit organization in 1999. Eventually, after a few years of local success, SCRAP Creative Reuse launched a grassroots network of creative reuse centers around the country. The key to their sustainable success was the development of a business model that could be shared and replicated.

The model SCRAP developed was centered on upcycling, repurposing, and otherwise giving products new life, a practice the founders called creative reuse. An old CD can acquire new value as an ornament or a coaster, wine corks or rubber tires can be turned into bath mats, and t-shirts from high school or a corporate retreat can be transformed into a quilt. Creative reuse centers like SCRAP collect discarded materials from the public that can be reused and made valuable to someone else through crafting. Many centers resell these items to the public or donate them to teachers or organizations for further reuse. This model creates a virtuous cycle for various stakeholders: educators can stretch their budgets, kids can become more environmentally conscious in a fun way, the local creative community is able to access inexpensive materials, thousands of pounds of useable materials are diverted from landfills, households, manufacturers, and businesses have a hub to donate unwanted materials (that would otherwise be dumped), and communities can create green-collar jobs.

The key to keeping this cycle going is to think carefully about the value propositions that keep reuse center customers not only coming into the center to buy materials but also donating materials and their time. Staff at the centers must design the marketing channels through which customers in their community can be reached while also considering which events will keep their volunteer staff interested. They must consider how to supplement grant funding with revenue not only from the sale of upcycled materials but also from the sale of materials like glue and paper, as well as packaged kits created for consumption at home. Thus, despite its nonprofit status and partial reliance on grants and donations, SCRAP was able to grow because it diversified its revenue streams and systematically put together a scalable and repeatable business model.

5.2 Orientation: Modeling Your Business

In previous chapters you did a lot of work to validate that individuals who fit your persona hypothesis need your solution. But founding a business involves more work than achieving persona-job fit. A lot of the "secret sauce" that makes for a successful startup may have nothing to do with the solution you are selling or whom you are selling it to and may instead concern how components of your business model come together. A **business model** describes the building blocks of an organization that are necessary for it deliver value, as well as to make or raise money.[1] Airlines, for example, sell tickets to seats on similar airplanes built by a handful of manufacturers. By and large, the solution sold by these companies is an equivalent A-to-B trip to largely similar destinations. Nevertheless, the way in which different airlines leverage assets, invest in resources, build partnerships, reach customers, and charge customers are wholly different. Southwest Airlines, for instance, focuses a lot of its effort on warm, personal service and no-frills conveniences (e.g., first two checked bags travel free) that align with the company's value propositions and are supported by training and marketing activities.[2] Southwest's secret sauce is not a feature of the product or service but the result of interdependent building blocks carefully interwoven to deliver on a value proposition (figure 5.1). It takes a lot of skill and foresight to build a business model that keeps pace with fast-changing customer demands and is difficult to imitate.

In this chapter, we turn our attention to the business model that underlies your startup. We describe each building block of your startup and specify how those building blocks work together

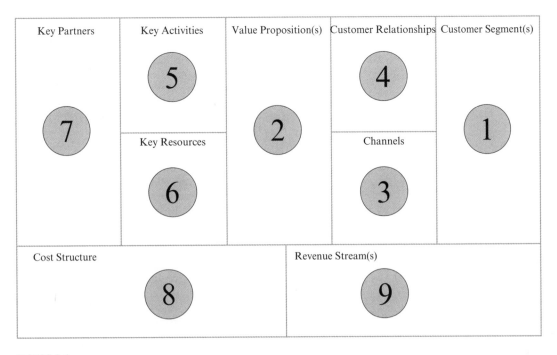

FIGURE 5.1
Business Model Canvas.
Source: Strategyzer.com.

to deliver value to your customer. To organize and visualize these building blocks, we use a tool that has become widely adopted in entrepreneurship circles after its introduction by Alexander Osterwalder and Yves Pigneur: the Business Model Canvas (BMC).[3] It used to be that when founders tried to explain what their startup was to audiences—including their own founding teams—they experienced a variety of communication challenges. These included talking past each other because their idea of what made up a business model differed, or overwhelming audiences with details that did not need to be discussed early in the new venture development process. While some founders talked only about customers, others emphasized the efficiency of their operations. This meant that people were not on the same page regarding what a business did, how it planned to do it, and what aspects of the business were key to delivering value.

To get around this issue, Osterwalder and Pigneur created a one-page canvas that allows all stakeholders to see which pieces of the organization are being highlighted. It is a good alternative to having everyone read an eighty-page business plan. There are nine building blocks in the BMC, each containing important information about one aspect of the business. If it helps you, you can think of these blocks as agreed-upon elements that together make up the outline of a business plan. If, on completion of the BMC, all blocks are well thought out and work together in concert, a founder will likely find they have formed a solid hypothesis of how to run an organization. And if anyone ever requests a business plan from you, the BMC building blocks can become useful headings. Because it is easy to understand and share, not because it is comprehensive (as were business plans popular in the past), the BMC has entered the entrepreneurship lingua franca (the common way people discuss new ventures) all over the world. To make the canvas easier to digest, I'll borrow from the design thinking toolkit[4] once again and split the nine-block canvas into three key business objectives common across businesses and crucial to success: (1) **desirability** (four blocks related to leveraging product-market fit and building excitement for your solution. By fiddling with these blocks, you can make or break your customer's interest in engaging with your business); (2) **feasibility** (three blocks that elaborate on what the business will need to deliver value to customers consistently. Time spent on this objective should yield a business that is better able to stay true to promises made to customers); and (3) **viability** (two blocks that focus on how all the activities and resources specified in the aforementioned blocks will be financed. The focus of these blocks is on how the business will generate money and what costs it will incur in delivering value) (figure 5.2). The grand hypothesis of the BMC is that if your business scores highly on these three key objectives, it will be efficiently delivering the most value to customers while maximizing profits.

Going forward, I will refer to the customer-facing parts of the business (those typically visible to or directly relevant in customer interactions) as the *front stage* and the parts that make the performance of the front stage possible (the operational aspects that support the front stage) as the *back stage*. I deliberately avoid using terms related to functional areas like marketing and operations because at this point, every founding team member should understand and have a hand in developing every aspect of the BMC. Specializing

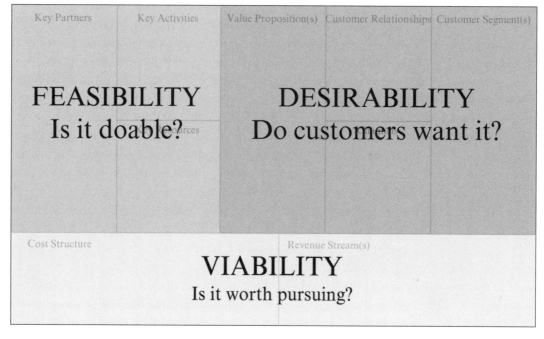

FIGURE 5.2
BMC Objectives.
Source: Strategyzer.com.

early may impede a true understanding of the interdependence of the building blocks of the business across the team. To illustrate all the building blocks of the BMC and how they are interdependent, I will adopt an easy-to-grasp example you should all be familiar with to some degree: the lemonade stand. Whether you ran a lemonade stand yourself as a kid or whether you have seen one in movies, the lemonade stand is a useful example because it is a simple retail model with a single revenue source. The working title for this twist on the lemonade stand concept is "Lemonation."

5.3 Business Model Canvas: Desirability

Customer Segments (1)   The first step is to identify a customer segment. If you have followed the steps in chapters 2 and 3, you have done a lot of this work already. For the sake of the running example in this chapter, however, I am going to ask you to think about a customer segment that fits the Lemonation concept. To place some limits on our imagination and keep our example straightforward, let's assume that I'm dead set on starting a lemonade business in a large urban park such as Central Park in New York, Audubon Park in New Orleans, Stanley Park in Vancouver, the Common in Boston, or a similar space. To make this example work in the small space we are allotted, we are limiting our initial beachhead to a large urban park that hosts activities ranging from jogging to dog walking to pick-up sports. A beachhead is the initial customer segment we are targeting as a business, so picking the right set of customers is crucial if we are to develop momentum early. We begin our exploration with some useful guiding questions: What kind of customers who frequent the park would be most interested in lemonade? How do we describe this group of customers so that it is specific enough to be useful when we start thinking about marketing and broad enough so that we have some wiggle room to make tweaks later? It helps to start thinking about the types of customers you typically see when you visit the park: joggers, parents with kids, older people strolling, cyclists. It seems that a lot of people visit the park to engage in activities that are healthy and fun. Why not capitalize on that? Let's aim our business at *health-conscious park visitors* who are likely to be thirsty after engaging in all these activities. They may also have children with them. And maybe they already buy food from mobile vendors when they are at the park. Notice I am trying to paint a rich picture of who these people are and why they might be at the park. Just as in the persona-crafting exercise, the richer the portrayal of the customer, the more likely we are to design a solution that is compelling to them.

Value Proposition (2)   Once we have a clear picture of who our potential customers are, we can start thinking about what we could do for them. What need would you address, or what job to be done would you tackle? A statement of the value you provide to customers is your value proposition. Different products and services provide different forms of value to customers. A customer looking for a sports car may compare a Ferrari and a Lamborghini based on performance or design, while that same person looking to insure that car may want to maximize risk reduction and confirm that the insurance company pays out reliably. Let us return to our lemonade stand targeting health-conscious park

FIGURE 5.3
Value Proposition Statement Diagram.

visitors. What solution would make sense for this segment of customers? I venture that they are thirsty and are looking for something refreshing. They probably do not want to stop exercising for very long or drink something that would erase any health gains they have made that day. With all that in mind, we can start hypothesizing features. Let's imagine we can sell a lemonade that is low in sugar or sugar-free, made with organic lemons, served ice cold, and served in a container that won't spill as people engage in exercise. That combination of product features fits the needs of the customers we are targeting. We could tell our customers that we are selling "ice-cold, lightly sweetened, organic lemonade on the go" (figure 5.3). Each of those words was carefully selected to convey features that deliver on a value proposition. By diagramming the phrase, we can start to understand which terms carry which message to potential customers:

Channels (3)   You now know the value your solution provides to a customer segment. But how will you reach these customers to tell them how great your product is? Where will the transaction take place? These questions have to do with how you plan to shape customer-facing channels, the means through which you will deliver value to a customer segment. Well-structured channels ensure that your perfectly crafted value proposition reaches the customer you crafted it for with as little loss of fidelity as possible. These value-delivery channels are often split into two types: (1) **marketing channels,** which generate awareness about your solution and ensure customers understand what you are selling and how it tackles a job to be done for them, and (2) **sales channels,** which have to do with where the transaction or the sale of the solution will take place and how it will proceed.[5] In our lemonade stand example, the marketing channels could range from brochures handed out in the park to an social media presence featuring high-resolution photos of organic lemons, or even highly visible signage attracting people to a booth in the park. The mix of marketing elements is based on what you think would best attract customers and propel their decision to buy.[6] The sales channel has more to do with easing or reducing friction in the transaction or purchase of the lemonade. Will you be a cash-only business or will you accept credit cards? Will you ask people to pay before they get their lemonade or after? These decisions may seem small in the grand scheme of things, but the time and treasure you spent building a customer's interest in your solution through your marketing channels can easily be undone by a long line at the lemonade stand or a frustrating payment system that isn't perceived as reasonable. Again, your best bet is to step into the shoes of potential customers and design what you think they would want to experience. With that in mind, it makes sense to review the Customer Journey Map you designed and mine it for ideal sales and marketing channel choices.

Customer Relationships (4)   Simply getting a customer to buy your product or service once is not enough to make most businesses successful. The customer relationship building block takes for granted that you can reach your customer through sales and marketing channels, but it does not specify the tools and tactics your business will use to retain customers over time. Businesses tackle maintaining relationships with their customers in a variety of ways, ranging from low-touch approaches used by companies creating automated solutions (e.g., vending machines) to high-touch approaches used by boutique hotels that cater to guests' every whim. Businesses may take advantage of promotions, coupons, and other discounting tools that boost a value proposition and draw customers back for another purchase. They may also support building relationships between customers through events or online communities, thereby encouraging individuals to remain connected to a business not just through a weekly newsletter or social media account but because they know their friends and acquaintances are also interacting with the brand. Whatever tool or tactic you select should align with other elements in the front stage of the business. For example, if your value proposition centers on exclusivity and status, using regular discounts or open events (rather than exclusive ones) may undermine the value that first attracted customers to your business. In our lemonade stand example we can use a compelling social media page and perhaps even a customer loyalty card whereby regulars can accumulate points and redeem them for a free lemonade as a means to keep people coming back. None of these techniques conflict with the refreshing, healthy, and convenient/portable value propositions the health-focused customers we are targeting find appealing.

Action: Leveraging the work you have done so far in earlier chapters, describe the four building blocks of the front stage of your business, that is, those that ensure your solution is perceived as and remains desirable. Try to balance being concise with explaining enough so that a naïve reader could understand exactly how value will be delivered to a customer segment through different channels and how the relationship with the customer will be not only maintained but strengthened over time.

1. Describe the **customer segment** you will be targeting initially (the beachhead):

2. Describe the core features of your solution (e.g., cold, organic lemonade) and the **value proposition** or propositions these core features convey (e.g., convenience, exclusivity):

3. Describe the **channels** (marketing and sales) you will use to reach out to and transact with your customer segment:

4. Explain the tools and tactics you will deploy to both maintain and strengthen **customer relationships**:

5.4   Business Model Canvas: Feasibility

Now that we have completed the front stage of our Lemonation business, let's look behind the curtain at the parts of the organization that make value delivery possible. Doing so will require us to take a break from thinking about shaping the customer's experience and start thinking about what it will take to ensure the consistent delivery of that experience day in and day out. In effect, it is time to consider how to make your business feasible.

Key Activities (5)   We can start by pinpointing what we need to do well as a company to deliver on every value proposition we promise and what we can outsource without damaging our value proposition. The key activities block describes the most important things a company must do to make its business model work. These activities form the basis of what will become the company's core competencies.* They are required to create and offer a value proposition, reach markets, maintain customer relationships, and earn revenues. The goal here is to determine what a company should excel at and where it can focus on being "good enough". An aspiring entrepreneur might claim that they wish to be the best at everything they do. A seasoned entrepreneur would say that doing so will likely lead to a diffusion of effort and attention, particularly given limited resources. The key is to go back to the value proposition and decide what you would like to be good at based on what you are promising to customers. Key activities differ depending on business model type and on how the front stage of the business is set. They can be categorized as (1) production, (2) problem solving, and (3) platform/network activities. Production activities relate to designing, making, and delivering a product in substantial quantities or of superior quality. Production activity dominates the business models of manufacturing firms. Problem-solving key activities relate to coming up with new solutions to individual customer problems. The operations of consultancies, hospitals, and other service organizations are typically dominated by problem-solving activities. Their business models call for activities such as knowledge management and continuous training. Business models designed with a platform as a key resource (e.g., eBay) are dominated by community and market-activity building. Networks, matchmaking platforms, software, and even brands can function as a platform. Key activities in this category relate to platform management, service provisioning, and platform promotion. Importantly, some organizations might have business models that rely on a mix of key activity types. Therefore, founders can use these categories as guides but shouldn't be afraid to create clever hybrids.

---

*Core competencies, a concept introduced by C. K. Prahalad and Gary Hamel, refers to the defining characteristics that make an entity, such as a business or an individual, stand out among rivals. They are strengths on which competitive advantage can be built (see Prahalad and Hamel, "The Core Competence of the Corporation," *Harvard Business Review* 68, no. 3 (1990): 79–91.

Since we are promising refreshing, healthy, and convenient lemonade, we can ask ourselves: What would we need to be great at doing consistently to deliver on these value propositions? To support our claims of having a refreshing product, employees at our lemonade stand will need to deliver an ice-cold drink that is sweet enough but not overly sweet. Excessive sweetness might get in the way of the thirst-quenching properties of the product. To deliver an ice-cold drink of just the right sweetness, we need to ensure that employees know how to create a balanced drink that has enough ice to retain its coolness throughout the drinking experience but is not so filled with ice that it becomes watery or difficult to carry (remember, we also promised on-the-go lemonade). To achieve this, employees need to be trained well and the lemonade-making process must be well delineated to avoid errors. We also promised that our refreshing concoction would be healthy. This means that we must look at all our ingredients to ensure they are sourced properly, that water is filtered to high standards, and that customers buy into our health claims. This may involve growing our own fruit, or at least having contracts in place with trustworthy farmers. It may also involve sourcing spring water or filtering it at a certified facility. Finally, we promised on-the-go convenience and portability. As such, we need to make the juice quickly and ensure the cups we provide can be used by active people who are moving through a park. Speed of production may involve training, automation, and other activities that can become part of a deeper repertoire. Notice how the customers we are targeting shape the value propositions and the value propositions in turn shape the activities we are obsessed with getting right.

Key Resources (6)   The key resources building block describes the most important assets required to make a business model work. **Resources** are stocks or supplies of money, materials, staff, and other assets that can be drawn on to support the delivery of a value proposition. They are the arrows in our quiver. What are the resources we have on hand or will need to make the business work? Will you need a building? Will you need to program software? What kinds of employees will drive the main functions of your organization or the things that make it really stand out from competitors?

Resources can be tangible, such as machinery or personnel, or intangible, such as knowledge or brand names. Resources can be divided into the physical, intellectual, human, and financial wherewithal that is needed to make the business run well. Independent of how you categorize resources, it is important to understand how they are leveraged to support key activities and, ultimately, the value propositions promised to customers.[†] Different key resources are needed depending on the type of business model. Some business models call for financial resources and financial guarantees, such as cash, lines of credit, or a stock option pool for hiring key employees. Others call for machinery, land, and technologies. Patents and other forms of intellectual property are

---

[†]Jay Barney, a leading entrepreneurial strategy researcher, differentiates between physical capital resources (technology, equipment, the geographic location of a firm, and its access to raw materials) and human capital resources (experiences, relationships, and insights of individual managers and employees in a firm) (see Barney, "Firm Resources and Sustained Competitive Advantage," *Journal of Management* 17, no. 1 [1991]: 99–120).

often leveraged by businesses to help protect advantages that allow them to stand out in crowded markets. All these key resources can be owned or leased by the company or acquired from key partners.

Lemonation would require several types of resources before it could even begin operating as a business. For instance, it would need a physical, mobile vending site where employees could make and sell lemonade. Some machinery, such as an automated juicer, might be necessary to ensure employees could focus on sales rather than on the minutiae of squeezing lemons. Carefully specified recipes for juice and sales processes would need to be developed. Some of the more unique recipes or key ingredient combinations might be kept secret so that customers can only find their favorite drink at our business. Employees would need to be well trained, and licenses to operate a beverage business on public land (an urban park) would have to be obtained. The list would grow rapidly as new product lines (e.g., limeade) or new locations (e.g., a campus gym) are added. A useful exercise is to look at similar businesses (e.g., Orange Julius) and examine what resources they use in their routine operation.

Key Partners (7)   We have identified the key activities we must perform and the key resources we need to make it all happen. Is there anything we would be better off relying on others to do? Could we do something better if we partnered with another organization? The key partners block describes the network of suppliers and partners that make your business model work. You can think of partners as external entities that you can rely on to reach economies of scale (e.g., contract manufacturers, shipping companies), reduce operational risk (e.g., insurance companies, law firms), and help you access difficult-to-acquire skills or know-how (e.g., coding shops, accounting firms). The decision to partner is an important one because it is tied to what key activities you are going to focus on. As a business, you will not get better or gain unique competencies in things you do not take on yourself. By outsourcing, you are choosing to avoid a learning curve or investment of resources in favor of immediate access to capabilities.

In the case of Lemonation, we will likely contract with an accounting firm, we may use lawyers to set up a legal entity under which we can operate with less personal risk, and we may even hire graphic designers to work on our website and signage. We might also sign contracts with local farmers to ensure a steady supply of organic fruit or decide to grow the fruit ourselves. Once again, our decisions should be guided by our value propositions.

Action: Leveraging the work you have done so far in earlier chapters, describe the three building blocks of the back stage of your business, that is, the aspects that make delivering your value propositions feasible. Try to balance being concise with providing enough explanation that a naïve reader could understand exactly how you will engage in key activities by drawing on resources or choosing to rely on trusted partners.

1. Describe the key **activities** you will focus on as a business to ensure you deliver on your value propositions:

2. What **key resources** will you need to have in place to support your key activities?

3. What are the **key partner** relationships you will need to develop to cover any activities you might not perform yourself or resources you might not have on hand?

5.5   Business Model Canvas: Viability

It is exciting to think about the different aspects of your business. Unfortunately, acquiring resources and performing value-producing activities will result in costs. Any business model worth its salt must include a full-throated discussion of costs, as well as revenue sources that will not only cover but reliably exceed costs.

Cost Structure (8)   When trying to understand the costs incurred by a business, it is helpful to think about the different categories or types of costs involved. The cost structure describes all the costs incurred to allow for the delivery of value propositions through the operation of a business model. The first costs to consider are startup costs. This is the money you will need to spend to get the business off the ground before you make your first sale. Legal fees and fees for design services, printing services, uniforms, and training are often incurred before an employee meets their first customer. Fixed costs are the more predictable costs that do not increase every time you make a sale. For instance, it does not matter how many lemonades I sell; the biweekly salary I pay my employees will not change, and neither will the fee I pay to the city to allow me to sell lemonade in the park. Variable costs, on the other hand, increase every time I make a sale. When I sell a lemonade, I am down a certain number of lemons, a cup, napkins, and even a paper receipt from the credit card reader. These things cost money and should be accounted for as variable costs.

Revenue Streams (9)   It has probably been a bit disconcerting to have to think about accruing costs without understanding how much money will be coming into the business with every sale. How much are customers willing to pay you for the value you provide and the special way you provide it? How do you make money? Your revenue streams are the sources of income you will have early in your startup's journey. The revenue stream for a lemonade stand is typically based on the lemonade sale transaction. But other streams are also possible: you could sell a subscription to an all-you-can-drink lemonade club instead of charging folks for every lemonade they buy (i.e., a Netflix for lemonade). You could also charge other brands to place ads on your lemonade stands or your lemonade cups if it does not turn off your customers. It is important to think carefully about the possible alternative revenue streams you can access and consider whether they align with your value propositions.

Action: Leveraging the work you have done in earlier chapters, describe the cost structure and revenue streams building blocks. Try to balance being concise with providing enough explanation that a naïve reader could understand exactly where you will be spending money and how you will be making it.

1. Describe the different items in your business's startup, fixed, and variable **cost structure:**

2. Explain what **revenue streams** will support your business (I suggest focusing on a single revenue stream early on if possible, to keep things simpler to manage):

5.6   Route Monitoring: Ensuring Business Model Coherence

Now that you have created a complete version of your business model, let us look back and see whether the building blocks come together in the most sensible way possible. To do this, we must stop thinking in terms of building block elements and start thinking about the relationships between the building blocks. Consider the front stage of the business. These are the building blocks that must work together to make people want to buy whatever solution you are selling. To work properly, the customers you describe must crave your value proposition. You should know that this is the case by now because you have done interviews to validate that relationship. However, for the value to be delivered to the customer and for the customer to keep coming back, you need the other two building blocks. In short, there should be a coherent, frictionless flow between the building blocks in the front stage (figure 5.4).

The same notion applies to the back stage of the business. Are the activities you describe related to the resources you list as important? Do those activities feed the value proposition or are they directed at delivering value you do not promise and that customers are

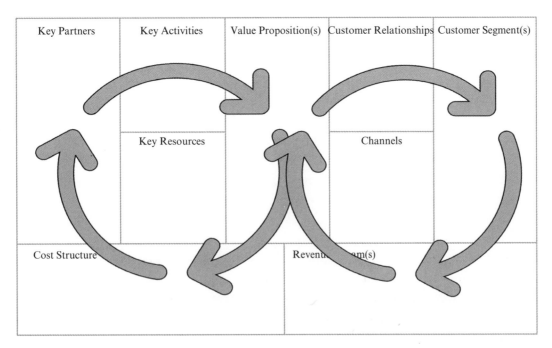

| Key Partners | Key Activities | Value Proposition(s) | Customer Relationships | Customer Segment(s) |

FIGURE 5.4
Business Model Canvas Coherence.
Source: Strategyzer.com.

not interested in? And do not forget about your partnerships. Is there a clear boundary between what activities the partners are performing and what you chose to make your core competencies? Finally, consider your costs and revenues. The costs should flow from your activities and the acquisition of key resources. Check to see whether the costs you list relate to the things you are supposed to be doing well. If they are not, consider whether those costs can be reduced or the activities that generate those costs outsourced to partners who might do them more cheaply. Revenues should fit with the flow of your front stage and make the offering more exciting. If the price or revenue model you selected is a huge source of friction that is making customers choose not to pull the trigger, you must go back to the drawing board.

5.7 Destination: Reflection and Next Steps

Founders who design their business using the BMC do not typically settle for the first version that comes together as a coherent whole and resonates with a customer segment. As a business grows beyond its beachhead market or as trends change, founders must remain agile and revise different building blocks to fit new conditions. This is as true of a lemonade stand that decides to expand beyond selling to health-conscious urban park-goers as it is of your business. The only static business model belongs to businesses that either never launched or failed to adapt to changing times. Here are a few things you can consider doing to ensure your business remains agile:

· Make the revision or tweaking of your BMC part of your founding team's routine by setting a monthly meeting at which data gathered from customers are used to challenge or reinforce hypotheses made in the BMC. Many businesses make a large version of the canvas, hang it on an office wall, and use sticky notes that are easily removable to ensure that founding team members and employees understand that even the most fundamental aspects of the business can be changed if the market demands it.

· Make different members of the founding team advocate for desirability, feasibility, and viability during BMC meetings so that any changes to your canvas do not sacrifice a pillar of the business.

· Your closest competitors are also changing the way they do business all the time. Consider creating and updating canvases for competitors or potential rivals that might clue you into their strategic moves before they upend your business. If your competitors pivot, make sure to understand what they did and why!

· Consult the resource page on the MIT Press website (https://mitpress.mit.edu/massa-wild). Content related to this chapter can be found under Founder Resources/Chapter 5.

6 Positioning Your Solution

Objectives

- Select a market entry strategy that considers the competitive dynamics in your beachhead market.
- Understand how features of your solution and the value propositions they convey allow you to stand out in a crowded market.
- Take stock of the macro factors and trends that may impel or hinder the advancement of your business.

6.1 Mini Case: Where to Dig

The idea first came to Casey Isaacson after a guy she was dating in New York refused to let her dog Layla into his apartment. Casey did not want to have to sort through suitors to find someone who would not have any hang-ups about her dog. So, she partnered with her sister Leigh to create Dig—The Dog Person's Dating App. The idea was to bring together "dog people"—anyone who cared deeply about dogs. The sisters hypothesized that unlike your standard dating prospect, who may or may not be on an app to find a relationship, dog people have the capacity to commit to and be responsible for another being. In other words, they are the ideal match for someone looking for a loving, long-term commitment: "To dog people, it doesn't matter who starts the conversation, what mutual hobbies they have, or who they know in common. If the people are not on the same page about the dog, they just aren't compatible." In short, Casey and Leigh knew the kind of users they were targeting and the job to be done they were tackling for them.

Market research, validation interviews with people who matched their persona, and conversations with experts on online dating went well, helping them tweak their idea and build out different components of Dig. They found, for instance, that 15 percent of US adults reported using multiple online dating sites or mobile dating apps and that the number was growing rapidly. Online daters used three to four dating apps for nine to ten hours a week, some of them calling online dating "a part-time job," for better or for worse. The same promising trends were present in their research on dog ownership among single, college-educated millennials, their target demographic. These millennials were at the age when they typically got their first dog and were exposed to a lot of dog-related content online. Their interviewees seemed to care about the quality of the dating pool in the app, how natural the matching experience was, and if people were in the app for the right reasons. One potential snag was that people in their target demographic had subscription fatigue. That is, they did not want to dish out money for yet another dating app. These data helped show them the kind of solution that they could build to really impress their users. Before investing much more of their time and money, however, they needed to understand more about the industry they wanted to break into, online dating.

At the time, the online dating market had gone through a wave of consolidation. Companies like the Match Group (owners of Match.com and Tinder) went on acquisition sprees, building portfolios of dating websites and apps targeting a variety of demographics. Smaller players created solutions targeting niche categories such as farmers, single parents, and sports enthusiasts. To say the market felt crowded was an understatement. New entrants and established players were advertising aggressively to garner the attention of active users, and every year new players entered the fray. How should Dig position itself in this market? What was the best way for the founders to introduce themselves to their potential customers?

Research on potential users and existing competition for their attention shaped their approach. They operated based on knowledge gained from validation interviews: a dating app is helpful only if it gives you plenty of choices in your area and eases the fear of meeting someone for the first time. To make this happen, they needed to ensure their app was populated with quality daters as quickly as possible. Casey and Leigh set out to create a powerful word-of-mouth engine. They began by attracting press attention with branded dog-friendly events in high-density urban markets (e.g., New York, Portland) which, in turn, drew the attention of dog community partners (e.g., dog costume designers, pet shelters) that eagerly promoted Dig on their own social media. The Dig team fed this cycle with targeted ads on social media featuring cute dogs and dog puns. Their most successful one was a picture of a cute dog available for adoption with the caption, "My mom is single." Because much of the buzz was self-sustaining and awareness of their brand was high, the amount of money they spent to enroll users was far below the industry average. They focused on rapid yet focused growth that made their app as useful as possible quickly and built them a rabidly loyal community. In this way their marketing strategy boosted their value propositions by ensuring a high-quality dating pool comprising people who had a lot in common with each other.

To balance keeping the app free to users without overwhelming them with irrelevant ads, the team made sure that advertisements were pet related. After all, these people were on Dig to meet people *and* to see cute dogs. The combination of being free to users and an intuitive ad-based revenue model would soon make them not only a growing business but one of the best-rated dating experiences on the internet.* It was only after the Dig team understood their users and their external environment—including trends (online dating, dog ownership), competitive dynamics (where their competitors fell short and where their strengths were), and how to leverage their advantages to build community—that the dating app started gaining traction.

6.2   Orientation: Positioning Your Solution

Even though you may have spent considerable time designing the building blocks of your business, your work defining the many aspects of your business is far from over. In fact, good founders constantly tweak their business model as new trends emerge and old ones fall away, as new rivals enter the fold, and as regulations change. The practice of routinely scanning one's environment and adjusting one's business model should not be the domain of resource-rich businesses. A big advantage that smaller businesses have over larger ones is their ability to quickly reallocate resources and do what experts refer to as **pivoting**.[1] One can pivot one or several of the building blocks of the Business Model Canvas, reconceptualizing a chunk of the business in the process.

A Successful Pivot

Andrew Mason envisioned a social platform where people could get together to rally behind social and charitable causes. The Point gained some decent traction when it launched in Chicago, but then started to fizzle. As an extension of the platform, the team added a subdomain—*Groupon*—whereby customers could pool their money to try to negotiate a group discount. That idea was far more popular, so the founders stuck with it and made it the central platform, expanding with opportunities for businesses.

Decisions to pivot are often triggered by punctuated changes in a company's external environment. Awareness of these changes can mean the difference between a business that is poised to capitalize on upcoming trends and one that is about to be crushed by waves of change. And while I have suggested aspiring founders focus on understanding their customer persona by zooming in for a rich and actionable picture, it is as important to zoom out and maintain **strategic vision**.[2] Luckily, there are many tools available to help founders visualize their external environment and make smart decisions regarding the future direction of their business. These include classics ranging from Michael

---

*Dig was invited to join the Internet Dating Excellence Association (IDEA) and won the backing of top brands like Purina. Cofounder Leigh D'Angelo was featured as one of the top twenty-four most influential people in the dating industry worldwide by Global Dating Insights.

Porter's Five Forces framework[†] to SWOT analysis[‡] and PEST analysis. *In this chapter, we borrow from the work of scholars and practitioners who created and improved on positioning tools over time to help founders develop a comprehensive view of their dynamic, external environment and adapt to it.* That is, while founders cannot control industry-level and even more macrolevel factors, they can shape a market positioning strategy that should help them thrive in a market or avoid it altogether.

6.3   Step 1: Picking a Market Entry Strategy

Markets differ in various ways: some are packed with competitors, while others seem like "blue oceans,"[§] unexploited by entrepreneurs and, at least for the time being, free from rivals.[3] In either case, or in any market entry situation, for that matter, it is important that entrepreneurs think strategically about how they will position themselves. A good market position will allow you to deliver as much value as possible to a growing market of customers while extracting lots of profit.

The *Entrepreneurial Strategy Compass*, developed by Gans, Scott, and Stern, helps guide entrepreneurs as they try to pick their market entry and positioning strategy.[4] The authors conceptualize the setting of a market entry strategy as being largely based on the two trade-offs described below:

- **Collaborate or compete?** A key decision a founder entering a competitive market must make is whether to be a partner of or a competitor to established players. That is, one can take part in any market as an alternative to existing solutions or as a complement to existing solutions. By collaborating with established players, a new entrant can gain access to knowledge, financial resources, preferential contracts, and other important determinants of market entry success. To recast this trade-off as a familiar metaphor, the battle between David and Goliath can be avoided if, instead of using a sling against Goliath, David offers to become his squire. And while collaborating may seem like a less romantic and perhaps inferior position to that of the young upstart, gaining support and protection from a giant may be the most efficient path to delivering

---

[†]The highly influential Five Forces model or framework was created by Michael Porter, a Harvard professor, as a heuristic to help manager determine the attractiveness and likely profitability of a given industry. He identified five forces that make up the competitive environment, and which can erode your profitability: (1) rivalry; (2) supplier power; (3) buyer power; (4) threat of substitution; and (5) threat of new entrants (Porter, "The Five Competitive Forces That Shape Strategy," *Harvard Business Review* 86, no. 1 [2008]: 25–40).

[‡]SWOT analysis (or the SWOT matrix) is a strategic planning technique used to identify strengths, weaknesses, opportunities, and threats (SWOT) related to a business venture (David W. Pickton and Sheila Wright. "What's SWOT in Strategic Analysis?," *Strategic Change* 7, no. 2 [1998]: 101–109).

[§]In an established industry, companies compete for every piece of available market share. The competition is often so intense that some firms cannot sustain themselves. This type of industry describes a red ocean, representing a saturated market share bloodied by competition. Blue oceans offer the opposite. Many firms choose to innovate or expand in the hopes of finding a blue ocean market with uncontested competition. See W. Chan Kim and Renée Mauborgne, *Blue Ocean Strategy, expanded edition: How to Create Uncontested Market Space and Make the Competition Irrelevant* (Boston: Harvard Business Press, 2014).

value to customers. This approach is not free of potential downsides. Entrants who turn out to be unskilled at maintaining their partnerships with an incumbent with greater bargaining power or who get mired in the same bureaucracies that prevent the large player from innovating in the first place may end up stymied before they even sell their solution. Other dangers include incumbents taking over your business or preventing your solution from reaching the market so that they can extract more profit from their own outdated market offerings.

Alternatively, competing against well-resourced incumbents can mean founders have the freedom to experiment with solutions and to target whomever they want as customers, particularly those the incumbent has overlooked or deemed too niche. The risk in being a "disruptor" is that a large incumbent might direct resources to squeezing you out of the market before you gain a foothold. It may, for instance, imitate your solution and use its well-known brand to take the air out of a promising avenue for marketing your solution.

- **Build a moat or storm a hill?** A related decision that can shape a business's market entry strategy relates to whether a founder chooses to play defense or offense. Some founders find that their best bet for successful market entry is to fortify themselves so that competitors cannot imitate their solution (e.g., an innovative process or technology). To build a moat around their solution, they often seek formal intellectual property protection or other legal means to exclude direct competition. Building this moat can, however, be expensive, particularly for an under-resourced startup whose biggest asset is typically an innovation that is not market tested. If founders choose this approach, they must rush to meet legal requirements for patent protection and keep a watchful eye for imitators who might choose to ignore legal protections.

  The alternative is to move quickly to market, gaining market share and brand equity quickly before competitors can usurp your market position. To "storm the hill," startups typically experiment with ideas while going to market and take on investment to speed up development and commercialization. Whereas the moat approach focuses on delaying new entrants and encumbering imitators, founders storming a hill rely on their agility to go through more iterations and gain the trust of customers before sleeping giants have a chance to respond. To quote Facebook founder Mark Zuckerberg: "Move fast and break things. Unless you are breaking stuff, you are not moving fast enough."

  As figure 6.1 indicates, in making the choices outlined above you are taking a first step on one of four distinct paths. Gans, Scott, and Stern refer to these paths as strategies. If founders choose to *collaborate* with incumbents, they may do so by (1) integrating their solution into an existing **value chain** owned by incumbents or (2) gaining **intellectual property** that is defensible and finding a way to integrate it into an existing marketplace in coexistence with incumbents. If founders choose to *compete* directly with incumbents, they can either engage in **disruption** by targeting customers ignored or underserved by the incumbents or they can make an **architectural** innovation play by creating an entirely new value chain that makes the existing way of doing things favored by the incumbents devoid of value to customers.

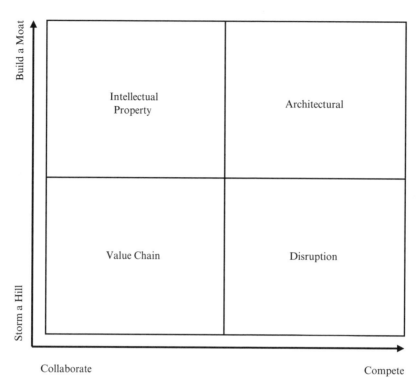

FIGURE 6.1
Entrepreneurial Strategy Compass.

Action: Apply the *Entrepreneurial Strategy Compass Framework* to determine what strategy you will embrace for your burgeoning startup. Based on the current and forecasted dynamics of the market you plan to enter, decide the following questions: (1) Is it more advantageous to compete or to collaborate with incumbents? (2) Is it more advantageous to build a moat or storm a hill? Based on these two decisions, name one of the four strategies you will adopt, and detail your rationale for selecting it:

6.4   Step 2: Taking Stock of Alternatives and Rivals

A founding team needs to fully understand the value propositions available to customers in the beachhead market being targeted, independently of whether those propositions are being offered by traditional competitors. Let's begin by examining industry-level factors that are often thought of as threats from existing competitors but may include threats from new entrants and potential substitutes.

If you were thorough when going through idea generation (chapter 2), you probably have a fairly good idea of the major competitors in your industry. You might have also captured alternatives being used by potential customers when conducting interviews or creating a customer journey map. It is now time to bring all that information together and add some depth to your picture of current and upcoming rivals. If we go back to our example of Rahul, the busy out-of-towner, and the Friendline website, we can examine how a founder might go about considering various potential rivals. Some alternative ways busy Rahul might make friends include joining local sports leagues, dating sites, or professional organizations, doing volunteer work, and so on. By Googling sites or apps to make friends, one might notice a trend: dating sites are getting into the friend-making business too (e.g., Bumble BFF, Tinder Social). There are also some newer offerings, such as Atleto, an app to help sport aficionados meet each other, Dig, the app designed to help dog lovers meet each other, and even Skout, an app that seems to do exactly what Friendline wishes to accomplish.

Your search should not end there because entrants in the pipeline—essentially, companies that will be entering the market soon—are also important alternatives that might be available to customers when you launch Friendline. A quick search of websites such as AngelList and Crunchbase—that is, sites specializing in aggregating startups looking for or receiving funding—reveals several new startups in the "friend-making" category (e.g., Patook, Sup, Status, Partywith). As you continue searching, consider how these different offerings fit into categories. Putting different alternative solutions into easy-to-understand and easy-to-communicate "chunks"[¶] can help you make sense of a crowded and dynamic market and is often the first step toward understanding where your startup will fit into the picture.[5] Some categories that emerge from the Friendline example include dating apps extending into friendship, hobby-based meeting apps focused on sports, pets, and other more niche interests; there are some that are focused on connecting solo travelers, and there is even one that uses artificial intelligence to ensure that people are using the app to make platonic connections and not romantic ones.

[¶]Chunking is a construct conceptualized by cognitive psychology to describe a mental process by which individual pieces of an information set are broken down and then grouped together in a meaningful and coherent whole (i.e., a category). People use chunking to group things into sets that are easier to understand, remember, and compare, thus bypassing the limited capacity of working memory. (See Fernand Gobet, Peter C. R. Lane, Steve Croker, Peter C. H. Cheng, Gary Jones, Iain Oliver, and Julian M. Pin, "Chunking Mechanisms in Human Learning," *Trends in Cognitive Sciences* 5, no. 6 [2001]: 236–243.)

Action: In table 6.1, list current and potential alternative solutions in rank order, starting with the one you perceive as the biggest threat to your business. Include both established companies and upcoming startups, as well as cobbled-together solutions, and alternatives used by potential customers in your beachhead market. Briefly explain the value proposition that is central to each alternative (i.e., does it sell convenience, ease of use, value, design, status?). These value propositions, as we have discussed in previous chapters, are the primary, underlying benefits that the company is trying to sell to customers. For instance, in women's fashion two value propositions that customers care about and fashion labels attend to are *value* (the cost-to-quality ratio that would tell me if a piece of clothing was a good buy) and something often referred to as *fashionability* (how hip or trendy a brand's collection is). Finally, list what about your proposed solution makes it superior to the alternative you listed.

Now that you have compiled a list of alternative solutions available to your customer, it is helpful to visualize how these alternatives relate both to your proposed solutions and to each other. That is, which alternatives are, from the customer's perspective, most like your solution, and how do they cluster together in the minds of your personae?

Perceptual mapping is a diagrammatic technique used by marketers to visually display the perceptions of potential customers. Typically, the position of a company's product, product line, or brand is displayed relative to its competition. **Perceptual maps**, also

Table 6.1 Alternative Solutions (Blank)

Name of Alternative	Brief Description of Alternative's Value Proposition	Why Your Solution Is Better Than This Alternative
1		
2		
3		
4		
5		

known as market maps, usually have two dimensions but can be multidimensional; they can be used to identify gaps in the market and potential partners or merger targets, and to clarify perceptual problems with a company's product.[6]

In the friend-making app market, customers like Rahul might care about such things as how naturally the interactions that lead to friendship progress, how easy it is to discover friends with desired traits, how easy it is to filter out unwanted advances from individuals not interested in platonic relationships, and even how curated or targeted the people shown as potential friends might be during the friend discovery phase. Based on some early conversations with Rahul, we find that he really cares the most about how *natural* (not forced or awkward) the relationship building is and how *easy* it is to make promising (auspicious) matches in terms of shared interests and a desire for platonic relationships. This information is useful because it can help us focus on which competitors Rahul, the busy out-of-towner, would select over others. Other personae might favor different value propositions, so it is important to go through these exercises for different personae, one at a time.

After downloading different applications and cataloguing the features that differentiate each offering, the Friendline founding team can create several visual representations that give an overview of how their startup is positioned relative to alternatives. And as figure 6.2 shows, they are also able to categorize these alternatives into clusters that occupy different spaces in the market. Note how some platforms, such as Peanut, a friend-making app for moms, occupy two different clusters—for Peanut, Interest-based and Gender-based.

After the team builds this perceptual map, the big question becomes, where will your solution thrive? There are various ways to approach the decision of where to position the app. How big are the markets in play, and is one of these markets still underserved? Is there a customer group whose needs have been ignored and that would make for a promising beachhead? This thinking was likely what led to the founding of the gender-based friend-making app companies. One might also ask: Are the companies populating this market doing a good job of solving the problem or are they failing in some (or several) aspects?

Based on this series of questions and on my ongoing conversations with potential customers that match the Rahul persona, I found that a common bridge between people is food. It is easy to start conversations with people that have similar tastes, even if you are a busy out-of-towner like Rahul (not to mention that out-of-towners often want to know the best places to eat). With this finding in mind, I decided to make my first pivot: Friendline would go from being a generic friend-making app to becoming an interest-based platform that connects people through food called FunDine.

Action: Complete the positioning map in figure 6.3. Proceed by (1) entering two value propositions (e.g., convenient, easy-to-use, authentic, efficient, safe), one for each axis, that will help you differentiate between players in the market, and (2) entering the names

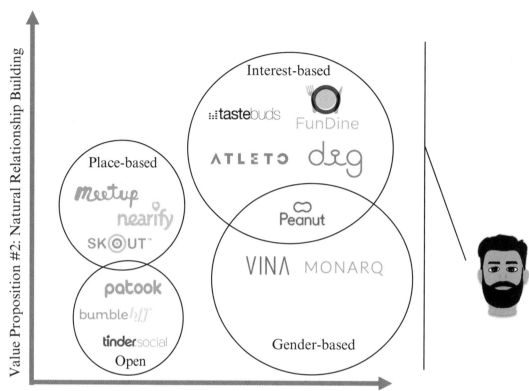

FIGURE 6.2
Friend-Making Perceptual Map.

of competitors into the area of the inner box that best aligns with how that competitor fits into the value proposition. Please include both direct competitors and any alternatives in use you may have identified already.

As you identify where to position your solution in this market and a handful of choices that personae might most closely associate as alternatives, you can begin to conduct other types of analyses. Many founders, for instance, choose to compare key features of their product to features offered by alternatives. An illustration of this often takes the form of a **feature comparison table**. I have created a version of the feature comparison table in table 6.2, where the top row lists three main alternatives to the new solution and the new solution and the first column lists features customers find most important. The cells often note whether this feature is present, or they may include a measure that helps potential customers distinguish between alternatives. It is important not to "oversell" your solution by picking weak alternatives or focusing only on features where you are strong. Try to create the best picture of the market alternatives that you can!

Action: Fill out a feature comparison table (table 6.3) contrasting your business with the top three alternatives for your primary persona. Be sure to focus on what is important to

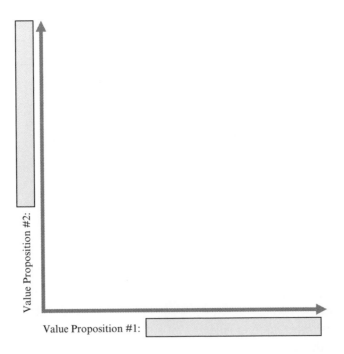

FIGURE 6.3
Perceptual Map (Blank).

your potential customers and not only on what makes your offering superior. Hopefully, you are superior across features that your customers value. If not, a redesign of your solution may be in order.

6.5 Step 3: Understanding Macro Factors

Alternative solutions are not the only factors hindering or advancing customer traction. One way to conceptualize the influence forces other than competitive dynamics might have on your business is to map and consider the current and future state of the macro environment. PEST** is an acronym for political, economic, social, and technological—external factors that commonly affect business activities and performance.[7] Created by Harvard professor Francis J. Aguilar in 1967,[††] the PEST framework can work alone or be used in combination with other tools.

- **Political.** Government regulations and legal issues affect any business's ability to be viable, feasible, or desirable. This factor of the PEST framework captures how that can

---

**There is overlap between PEST and SWOT, in that similar factors would appear in each. That said, PEST and SWOT are certainly two different perspectives: PEST assesses a market and its many underlying factors, including competitors, from the standpoint of business. SWOT assesses the relative tactical position of a business, whether your own or a competitor's.

[††] Aguilar's 1967 book, *Scanning the Business Environment* (New York: Macmillan), examined how companies acquire and use information about external events and trends to aid in strategic planning.

Table 6.2 Friend-Matching Feature Comparison

	Peanut	Atleto	Tastebuds	FunDine
Interest-Based Filtering	✓	✓	✓	✓
Gender-Based Filtering	✓	✓	X	✓
Natural Icebreakers	X	X	X	✓
Assurance of Platonic Relationships	✓	X	X	X
Matching Algorithms	✓ Based on quizzing/ mom matching	✓ Based on sports	✓ Based on taste in music	✓ Based on dining preferences

happen. Issues that must be considered include tax guidelines, copyright and property law enforcement, political stability, trade regulations, social and environmental policy, employment laws, and safety regulations. Founders might also consider their local and federal power structure and discuss how anticipated shifts in power could affect their business. For instance, tax incentives given to non-US competitors of FunDine may undercut its entire business model. Also, legislation restricting the use of online friend-making sites by minors could limit what markets are viable for FunDine.

- **Economic.** This factor examines the economic issues that can play a role in determining the trajectory of your startup. Items to consider include economic growth, exchange, inflation and interest rates, economic stability, anticipated shifts in commodity and resource costs, unemployment policies, credit availability, and unemployment policies. The unemployment rate and availability of disposable income to targeted customers may influence whether they choose to invest in making friends by using FunDine.

- **Social.** The social factor analyzes the demographic and cultural aspects of the company's market. These factors help businesses examine consumer needs and determine what pushes them to make purchases. Among the items that should be examined are demographics, population growth rates, age distribution, attitudes toward work, and job market trends. Social food trends may influence when and how FunDine users choose to meet and how they interact to create meaningful experiences.

- **Technological.** Technology issues affect how an organization delivers its product or service to the marketplace. Specific items that need to be scrutinized include, but are not limited to, government spending on technological research, the life cycle of current technology, the role of the internet and how any changes to it may play out, and the impact of potential information technology changes. Just as with other factors, companies should consider generational shifts and their related technological expectation to figure out how they will affect who will use their product and how it is delivered. Changes in matching algorithm technologies, discoveries in artificial intelligence, and other trends may influence how competitive FunDine can remain in a market built on propitious matching.

Table 6.3 Feature Comparison

	Alternative 1	Alternative 1	Alternative 3	Your Solution
Feature 1				
Feature 2				
Feature 3				
Feature 4				
Feature 5				

Action: Using the prompts listed in each factor category in table 6.4 as a starting point, fill in any relevant factors that might influence customer traction, acquisition, or discovery for your startup. Do your best to list each item in order of importance to your startup. These will be important when trying to understand opportunities and threats now and in the future.

6.6 Destination: Reflection and Next Steps

Now that you have completed an assessment of your competitive and macro environment, consider changes you can make to your business model and apply them to your BMC. Doing so will ensure that the research you have completed is not left unused, gathering dust on a shelf. You can also take the following steps to ensure you end up with a coherent business model that fits the external environment:

Table 6.4 PEST Analysis

Political factors:	Economic factors:
• Environmental issues that may influence the commercialization of your solution • The tendency of regulatory bodies to intervene in your industry • Government policies such as trade restrictions on limitations on the production of a particular solution • Public capital (e.g., grant) availability • Lobbying or pressure group priorities • Wars and crises (e.g., pandemics)	• Local or overseas economic busts or booms • Taxation issues • Seasonality or weather issues • Market and trade cyclicality • Specific industry factors • Logistical or distribution trends or prices • Customer/end-user drivers • Interest and exchange rates
Social factors:	**Technological factors:**
• Lifestyle, fashion, generational trends • Demographic trends • Shifts in consumer attitudes and opinions • Consumer buying patterns (e.g., online versus offline) • Buying access and trends • Ethnic or religious factors • Relevant vehicles for advertising and publicity • Ethical issues	• Consumer comfort with technology • Competing technologies now and in the future • Availability of research funding • Associated or dependent technologies • Replacement technology or solutions • Technological maturity of industry • Manufacturing maturity and capacity • Consumer buying technology • Intellectual property issues such as licensing, patents

- Identify and subscribe to industry publications, newsletters, online forums, and other "insider sources" that will help keep you abreast of changes in industry trends, technological advancements, and other important factors that might influence how you shape your business model.

- While keeping up with trends is an important aspect of a founder's job, it is important to avoid obsession. One of the best ways to stay ahead of trends is to stay in touch with your customers. If your value proposition still resonates, you will buy yourself some time to adapt to external shocks. Remember, keep a balance between zooming in to the customer experience and zooming out to take in the PEST factors and competitive landscape.

- Trends may affect industries differently. Some industries are immune to the ups and downs of fads and fashions, while others live and die on the latest and greatest. Gaining a deep, historically grounded perspective on your industry and how it behaves is often as important as developing a sensitive radar for key trends or customer preferences.

- Consult the resource page on the MIT Press website (https://mitpress.mit.edu/massa-wild). Content related to this chapter can be found under Founder Resources/Chapter 6.

Validating Your Solution

Objectives

- Focus efforts on developing a contact list and an interview protocol that will allow the validation of a solution.
- Capture and analyze results of the interviews to determine whether the current business model and minimum viable product resonate with personae the business intends to target at launch.

7.1   Mini Case: Trial by Fire

As the first black-owned brewing company in the South and the fifth in US history, Cajun Fire Brewing Co. had big plans and the energy of a proud community behind it. After founding the company in 2011, cofounders Jon Renthrope, Adam Dawson, Courtney Renthrope, Jomarque Renthrope, and Paul Taylor turned their attention to making beer with deep cultural roots. Flavors like Acadiana Honey Ale showcased the New Orleans melting pot, while others drew from African Diaspora and Houma Indian flavor profiles. The founders discovered that their customers were interested not only in drinking delicious craft beer but in being a part of a community. That is why, when trying to come up with the right recipes to brew, the team at Cajun Fire insisted on letting the customers weigh in, and included them in the development process. Team members spent much of their time giving away samples at festivals, block parties, pop-ups, and other events in exchange for customer feedback on their product and suggestions for new flavor profiles. Dawson put together a website that would not only collect emails from customers excited about a beer with New Orleans flavors but would also sell merchandise. After all, every t-shirt or beer glass sold online was a good indicator that people were interested not just in the beer but bought into their brand and mission.

To receive feedback on their business model, the team participated in several pitch competitions. That allowed them to hone their pitch and had the added benefit of providing them with significant cash infusions: they claimed the $50,000 prize as part of the Big Idea Pitch Competition at the finale of the annual New Orleans Entrepreneur Week. They used the buzz around their win to collect feedback once again on both their product, from customers who fit their target persona, and on their business model, from the best experts they could find. Taste tests, tests to validate the look and feel of beer cans, and tests to pinpoint the appropriate "hoppiness" and "maltiness" of each offering became part of the founding team's routine. The team was even hosted by the Smithsonian Museum of National History in Washington, D.C., at its annual food summit, where hundreds of people got to try Cajun Fire's products and one of its beers won the Best in Show award.

At the core of Cajun Fire's solution validation strategy were hundreds of conversations. Each beer the team develops is intentionally designed to satisfy a constituency and to help the team continue building up a fan base both within and outside the New Orleans community. Cofounder Jon Renthrope is proud to say that "reception has been exceptional. The company has been featured on more than 150 media outlets around the world."

7.2   Orientation: Validating Your Solution

You've done a lot of work to ascertain the existence and urgency of a particular job to be done, to identify the persona who might be most interested in paying to have this job tackled, and to outline the building blocks of an organization. You have not, however, completed the important work of receiving feedback on your *solution* and testing it with customers. A testable solution includes two interconnected parts:

1. **Business model:** A well-crafted rationale of how an organization creates, delivers, and captures value and makes money. In the startup world, this is usually shared with others through the *Business Model Canvas* (BMC).

2. **MVP** (Minimum Viable Product): A product or service with just enough features to satisfy early customers and to allow founders to gain useful feedback that will inform future product development.[1] The core of your offering, it addresses the most pressing job to be done for your early adopters, without any bells and whistles.

Focusing on validating features of your product or service or trying to determine what price to charge may be important steps. They will not, however, help you be sure you have a good business on your hands. For instance, you may have built a wonderful prototype that would be easy to manufacture and that tackles all your customers' major problems. You decide, without consulting your customers, to adopt a revenue model whereby you push customers to sign up for a subscription instead of paying a one-time fee. When you go to market, you may find that your product generates a lot of buzz, but customers are not pulling the trigger on the purchase because they are unwilling to commit to a subscription. In short, an MVP and a business model must be validated together because it is that combination (in its entirety) that will be sold to and considered by potential customers on their journey. This means that the combination of the BMC and the MVP makes a solution testable with customers.

This chapter guides you through the key steps you need to take to ensure that your solution is testable and that you properly deploy tools to test it. As you did when conducting opportunity validation, getting good information means that you have to talk to the right people and ask questions that allow customers to share both positive and negative feedback. The better the information you can gather at this point, the more likely it is that you will receive positive reviews when your solution launches.

7.3   Step 1: Listing Potential Interviewees

For many of you, the work of gathering a list of potential interviewees will be simple, particularly if your hypothesis about who your core persona is has panned out. However, if you had to pivot to a different beachhead, or if you found during your previous interviews that the job to be done was more pressing for a different persona, you'll have to conduct interviews with a completely new set of people. Typically, the solution validation interviews include a subset of the people you have already interviewed *and* a new set of people that match your latest best guess of who your core beachhead customer might be. Note that you should now be completely focused on interviewing potential customers that fit your persona hypotheses, not industry experts. Investors will expect several dozen interviews *at least*, as well as a sense that you have answered your validation questions fully.

Action: List potential interviewees that are great matches for your primary customer persona (table 7.1).

With this list in place, you can begin scheduling interviews. Try to allocate more time for these interviews than you did for the opportunity validation interviews. In my experience, these interviews may take more than forty-five minutes. They will take more time because you will be sharing your business model, showing your prototype or demo, and getting feedback on both. Please be sure to ask permission before recording interviews, take copious notes, and thank your interviewees for being generous with their time and insight, both in person and in a follow-up email. Remember that these interviewees may become your first customers and top evangelists when you go to market.

7.4   Step 2: Creating an Interview Protocol

Much as when you engaged in problem validation interviews, it is important that you create a protocol to structure your interview and to make sure all your teammates are

Table 7.1 Solution Validation Interviewee List

Customer Name	Job Title, Relevant Role, and Organization	Email/Phone
1 Roger Canseco	Purchasing Manager, ACME	Roger@acme.com / 555-5555
2		
3		
4		
5		
6		
7		
8		
9		
10		

on the same page. The protocol can be tweaked along the way and as you adjust your business model or MVP. Try not to get caught up in showing every detail of your product or business model. The focus should be on getting feedback on pieces of your testable solution that you think could use work or that are amenable to this kind of validation. Table 7.2 contains an abridged sampling of potentially relevant solution validation questions. Whether these exact questions are appropriate or not depends on the kind of business you are starting.

Action: Now it is your turn to try your hand at building your own solution validation interview protocol (table 7.3). Consider the first or second most promising person on your contact list. What kinds of questions do you need to ask them? How much time can they afford to give you? Make sure you leave at least three minutes for each response and have some follow-up questions prepared in case the person you are speaking with gives you short answers.

Once you have completed your protocol, be sure to rehearse the interview at least once with a friend. You may find that some questions do not sound quite right or that you are not getting the quality of responses you were expecting. If so, go back to the drawing board. Also, your protocol should change depending on how far along your business has come and your sense of how much evidence you have collected to support the hypotheses that underlie that business. The relevance and phrasing of your questions will largely determine the quality of the responses you receive.

Table 7.2 Sample Solution Validation Interview Questions

Category	Instructions	Sample Questions
MVP Validation	Ask these questions only when you are sure the customer is intrigued by what you are developing. Show the customer a prototype or use case, and be sure that they fully grasp what they are seeing.	• What do you think of this solution? What was the first thought that came to mind? Did your impression change after interacting with it? • In what circumstances might you use this solution? Why? • What might prevent you from using this solution? • When would you be willing to start using/implementing this solution? • What is most (least) appealing to you about this solution? • What would make you want to tell your friends about this solution? • What change might improve your experience using the solution? • Is there something I did not ask? Something I missed?
Business Model Validation	Ask these questions after customers have been able to see or use your MVP. Lay out the latest iteration of the BMC, explain the tool, and focus on a few key boxes. I suggest you start by validating the front stage of the business and getting to the back stage if you feel you have time.	• Channels: Would this be the best way to reach you? Would you like the sale to take place online or offline? • Customer relationships: What would keep you coming back? • Value propositions: Do you feel that these features and reasons make sense for why you would want this? How would you rank these in order of importance to you? • Revenue model: What would be the minimum you would reasonably expect to pay? the maximum? What price would be fair? How would you prefer to pay—in installments, by subscription, or all at once? • Partners: Whom do you think we should partner with to sell this product? What other products would you buy with this?

7.5   Step 3: Capturing Interview Results

Capturing interview results can be challenging. A few issues that can make the process more complicated than it needs to be include the following:

- You did not record or take notes during the interview, making it nearly impossible for you to remember key details that can influence what should change about your MVP or business model.

Table 7.3 Solution Validation Interview Protocol (Blank)

1
2
3
4
5
6
7
8
9
10

- Different versions of the MVP or Business Model are shown to different interviewees creating discrepancies between responses that make them difficult to contrast.

- The sample you selected does not really match the persona you currently believe should be in your beachhead market, making it likely that their idea of what makes a good solution is not what you have to showcase.

- The questions you asked were not well crafted to lead to rich, open-ended responses, leaving you with data that do not really tell you more than an online survey might.

Action: To help you organize and understand the results of your interviews fill out table 7.4 after each interview. If you interview more people than the number of lines provided, just keep going with a printed or handwritten version. I also recommend that you listen to a recorded version of the interview (obtained with the interviewee's permission) while you fill out the form. Begin by listing the name and role of the interviewee, the date, and how long the interview took from start to finish. Follow with lessons learned from the interview, such as counterintuitive insights that changed your mind about something important, new knowledge you gained from a story or response, or even an insightful quote that can be shared with investors and employees to illustrate an important point later. Finally, make a note of any changes you intend to make to the BMC or to your MVP based on what you learned from the interview.

This form should not be the only repository of data you maintain. It is meant to be filled out telegraphically and is designed as a way for you to communicate your findings with advisers or members of your founding team. Some teams generate many of these

Table 7.4 Solution Validation Interview Log

	Interviewee Name and Role/ Date and Time Spent	Lessons Learned	Changes to MVP or BMC
1	Interviewee Name: Role: Date: Time Spent:		
2			
3			
4			

forms and start categorizing their interviewees into persona categories, sometimes finding new and interesting potential markets in the process.

7.6   Step 4: Triangulating Findings using Alternative Validation Methods

While I have emphasized interviews as the chief means through which you might obtain information from experts and customers, several techniques have been developed and tested by entrepreneurs and scholars to help guide decision-making in early-stage start-ups. In what follows, I describe prominent early-stage, solution validation methods. The list is far from comprehensive, but awareness of how these validation tools and methods can complement interviews is important.

First is a **landing page**. Many early-stage companies prioritize buying a domain name and putting up a simple landing page or a website that conveys a well-crafted value proposition and allows visitors to express their interest in some sort of call to action. That is because a well-designed landing page coupled with some minimal, targeted advertising can rapidly yield a list of potential customers or even qualified leads. This list can be mined for interviews, crowd-funding campaigns, pilots, and so on. If successful, it can serve as its own form of solution validation when pitching to investors, though it is a somewhat trivial one. Importantly, it requires little investment of time or treasure. A company might, for instance, capitalize on specialized knowledge by offering potential customers a free guidebook. To obtain the free guidebook, the company could require that customers sign up for a newsletter using their professional email or that they create an account by linking a Facebook or LinkedIn profile.

You can also design **surveys**[*] and send them to potential customers on lists compiled through a landing page registry or through interview referrals. While interviews are useful for exploration and to ask open-ended questions, surveys are great for closed-ended questions or to increase the data points needed to validate a hypothesis. For instance, let us say we recently launched the third version of an MVP for an organic produce home delivery box called Bounty Box. We offered it to our mailing list, and, with purchase, we asked customers to fill out a short survey. We might ask ranking questions to ascertain why they chose to purchase (thereby strengthening our value proposition validation). We could also ask whether customers thought the box was a good deal, and adjust our pricing accordingly. Finally, we could validate channel choices and journey maps by asking where and how often customers typically buy produce.

Whether we are testing software or physical products, **A/B testing** is a great way to quickly get a sense of what customers really want.[2] A/B tests are experiments companies run to determine which versions of their products or channels work best. Visitors to a website, for instance, may be randomly distributed across alternative website versions that essentially perform the same function but have slight design differences. The version of the page that yields the most signups or purchases can be adopted based on the test.

Advertising, shared via posts or full-fledged profiles on Instagram or Facebook, can be easily used to validate aspects of the business model or to ascertain the appeal of an MVP, channel, or go-to-market strategy to targeted customer segments. Consider creating an ad that pushes potential customers to a landing site. A/B test different ads to ensure that your ad is resonating with the right audience and that all steps in in the customer journey are producing engagement.

Many tools are available to help you launch a business by spending very little money and making small bets. I suggest you play with as many of them as possible before launching your business. Notice also that each of these tools can strengthen the effectiveness or reach of another, so be sure to consider not just the worth of stand-alone tools but how they can be deployed in concert to validate hypotheses.

Action: Select one or two alternative validation methods and conduct an experiment that validates something about your solution. Feel free to get creative by using the methods I suggest above or leveraging your own ideas. In his book *Testing with Humans,* Giff Constable notes that startups get creative with experiments by, for instance, using the "Wizard of Oz" technique, whereby customers think they are interfacing with a real service or a fully built

---

[*]Several websites provide information and resources to help founders conduct market research and solution validation research. Because these are very distinct, depending on the market or industry a startup is entering, consider building your own survey using the appropriate resources.

product but in reality a team is delivering the solution in a manual way until the service delivery processes and customer needs are fully understood.[3] The goal for folks using the Wizard of Oz technique and for your venture is to get in the habit of trying things out before making large financial commitments. Report the findings of your experiment(s) below:

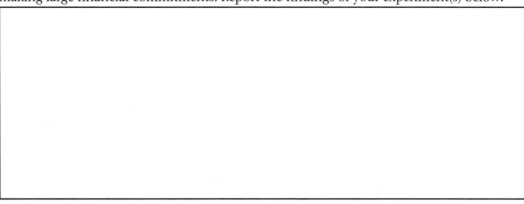

7.7   Route Monitoring: Interpreting Customer Data

Capturing a lot of data is critical to the entrepreneurial process. However, as experienced scientists will tell you, a large trove of data can be overwhelming and lead you in a lot of strange directions if it is not analyzed and interpreted systematically. Many tools are available to help you make sense of the data you've collected, but understanding often starts with conversations between you and the other members of the founding team who have been immersed in the interview process. The Progress-Making Forces framework[4] (figure 7.1) is one tool that can help you structure this discussion and direct it toward understanding the ins and outs of your potential customer's demand for your solution. It will also give you lots of insight into what it takes to change entrenched customer behavior.

The basic premise of the tool is as follows. For someone to transition from an existing behavior (a solution they are currently using) to a new, untested behavior (switching to a new solution), there are two types of forces at work: progress-making forces and progress-hindering forces. Progress-making forces propel people from their existing behavior to the new behavior and consist of the push of the current situation (things they're not happy

FIGURE 7.1

Progress-Making Forces.

Source: Adapted from http://jobstobedone.org.

with in the current solution) and the pull of the new idea (things that sound appealing about the new solution). Progress-hindering forces, on the other hand, hold people back from switching to new behavior. They consist of allegiance to the current behavior (things they really like about the current solution) and the anxiety surrounding adoption of the new solution (e.g., worries about learning curves and not being able to accomplish their goals with the new solution). For someone to switch from an existing solution to a new one, *the progress-making forces must be stronger than the progress-hindering forces*. Is the proposed solution that much better than a current solution? What does the new solution have to do to overcome people's allegiance to what they are currently using? If you have conducted lots of interviews already, it is likely that you will have some insight into what your potential customer concerns and motivations are already. If not, you might want to do more interviews.

Action: Based on information gathered in your problem and solution validation interviews, answer the following questions *for your primary persona*.

Push

How is my current solution affecting my life in ways I am not happy with?

```



```

Pull

How do I imagine the new solution will change my life for the better?

```



```

Anxiety

What uncertainties or concerns do I have regarding adoption of the new solution?

Allegiance/Habit

What position am I in today or what alternative do I have in place that negates the need to adopt a new solution?

7.7   Destination: Reflection and Next Steps

By the time you reach this marker, you should have many different sorts of data to validate that you are solving a real problem, for a real set of customers, in a way that is compelling to them. The time that elapses between now and when your startup launches, however, is a dangerous period. If you lose touch with your customers or if you slip back into a closed solution development process, you are likely to forget much of what you learned by engaging deeply with customers. The customer perspective should always serve as the North Star. But navigating by starlight is useless if you keep your head down. To keep your founding team aligned and following the path determined by customers, then, do the following:

- Continue conducting interviews and recruit a subset of straight-talking customers to become a sounding board for any modifications or additions to the solution. Easy access to these customers will allow you to develop and update solutions rapidly without sacrificing true customer insight.

- If it is helpful, think of your customer personae as an advisory group that sits on your shoulders. It may sound silly at first, but internalizing their voices and ensuring that their opinions are represented in founding team discussions can do wonders to help avoid myopic decision-making or groupthink.

- Consider the benefits of co-creation. You have had time to interview many different potential customers by this point. Perhaps some of them stood out as particularly insightful. Maybe some are buyers at large companies you could partner with to develop the solution in tandem. Hiring your most insightful customers or making development partnerships official can help assuage investor concerns and keep your product development process from going off the rails.

- Consult the resource page on the MIT Press website (https://mitpress.mit.edu/massa-wild). Content related to this chapter can be found under Founder Resources/Chapter 7.

8 Projecting Financials

Objectives

- Determine a revenue model that best fits your customer preferences and supports your business model.
- Price your solution using a variant of value-based pricing.
- Calculate the size and potential of the market you plan to enter.
- Project profits and losses for your venture in the twenty-four months that follow the launch date.

8.1 Mini Case: Financing Privy Label

After working for five years as a fashion designer for an international performance lifestyle brand, Jessica Osborn decided to build her own business. She leveraged her connections with US-based factories and her own fashion logistics expertise to help clothing brands all over the country create their own custom clothing lines. By contracting with Privy Label, up-and-coming brands could quickly gain access to an in-house design and development team that handled sketching, fabric sourcing, sample development, and manufacturing. It was a turnkey option for creatives who would otherwise have to spend lots of time and money figuring out contracts and processes.

The idea took off. Within a few months Jessica and her newly hired director of operations, Cristina Contreras, were having to turn clients away or put them on a waiting list. The only way to serve so many clients would be to pivot: to change the way they operated for scalability. After several strategy sessions, the team decided to study the possibility of creating an online platform that could handle a high volume of requests by connecting clothing brands directly with vendors that fit their needs. The Privy Label team wanted to create a carefully curated platform that would do the work Jessica did as an intermediary every day.

The first step the team took was to consider a revenue model. Should customers pay a subscription to access the vendors or should a fee be charged on transactions? How much should be charged? The hard work of interviewing customers and gathering data on customers' preferred way of paying for the services provided through the platform began. After dozens of interviews, Jessica and her team had an answer: the customers they were targeting needed to see all the vendors on the site and understand the value of access before they would be willing to pay. The fee would need to be charged on top of vendor fees for each transaction. The result would be a platform that was as convenient and curated as possible while still generating revenue for the startup. After all, a good revenue model should not stand in the way of a working value proposition.

8.2 Orientation: Projecting Your Startup's Financials

Most of the elements you will need to credibly explain what your business does to external stakeholders should be in place by the time you start putting together your financials. What might be lacking is easy-to-interpret evidence that shows these audiences that your business is financially viable. We have referred to *viability* earlier in the book (see chapter 5) when we tried to define a cost structure and revenue streams in the Business Model Canvas (BMC). Thinking about those building blocks was an important step to take, but it was insufficient. Many investors will want to know that you have done your best to forecast your venture's financial success by looking ahead at how much money you might spend and generate. After all, investors expect healthy returns and feel more comfortable if they have at least a ballpark sense of what you, the founder asking for money, believes is realistic.

In this chapter, you will use information you have gathered from customer interviews and other data sources to construct a rudimentary profit-and-loss projection for your startup. That projection will be based on a set of well-reasoned assumptions and conservative guesses whenever solid data are not available. Your aim will be to minimize risk while maximizing profit from each of your revenue streams. The goal of this exercise is *not* to create a complete, robust set of financial ("pro forma") statements but to begin making decisions regarding (1) how you are going to charge for your solution, (2) how much you will charge, (3) how big the market for the solution will likely be, (4) what the first twenty-four months of revenues might amount to, and (5) what costs will accrue in the first twenty-four months of the business's existence. This seems like a lot (and it is), but I hope that the simplified, step-by-step approach I provide here can make the process possible. To better help you, this chapter has a **companion Microsoft Excel™ workbook** available for download on the MIT Press book website (https://mitpress.mit.edu/massa -wild) under Chapter 8/Founder Resources. Use it to help you determine what you need to attend to when making "go" or "no-go" decisions regarding the financial future of your venture.

8.3   Step 1: Deciding on a Revenue Model

The revenue model you select is a key component of your business model and the means through which your business will attain financial objectives. It must be grounded in the characteristics of the market and customers you choose to serve. It should also consider the models of existing competitors, as well as ongoing trends in the broader external environment. When selecting your revenue model, consider the following: (1) Is it consistent with how, in an ideal world, your customer would want to purchase your product or service? (2) Does it enhance or detract from your value proposition(s)? For instance, if you are trying to sell your customers on a more convenient way to perform a task, making it time-consuming to research and purchase a product would be counter to your value proposition. (3) Will adopting this revenue model now make your business sustainable in the future? For example, some companies attempt to give away their solution for free at the outset to drive adoption and build a critical mass of customers, but then are abandoned by customers when investment money dries up and the business is pushed into charging for the solution. To help you search for a revenue model that fits your venture, I list a few options in table 8.1. The list is not comprehensive, but it includes some options that have become increasingly popular. Just as you did in the other chapters, keep your customer persona in mind when deciding the revenue model that is right for your venture.

Note that table 8.1 does not include options that are often adopted by non-revenue-generating organizations, such as grant- or donor-funded nonprofits. If that is the route you wish to take, consider how you might attract donor funds and frame grant proposals. It should be noted that grants and donations are not, in most cases, reliable sources of long-term funding, so I suggest that, if your product or service is amenable to such a thing, you consider some form of revenue generation to supplement and eventually supplant other forms of funding.

Action: Describe the revenue model you have selected for your venture. Explain why this model makes sense for the value proposition you are making and the preferred buying behaviors of your targeted customers:

Table 8.1 Descriptions of Revenue Models

Model	Description
Transaction-based	This model relies on a single transaction in which customers pay fully for a product or service. This allows the customer not to worry about long-term commitments and simplifies consideration by focusing the customer on a single business deal. If a product or service is very expensive, however, requiring customers to dish out the full amount in one shot can limit your customer base. Selecting this model may also mean that you must convince customers to buy into your value proposition every time you want to make a sale. Unlike your local gym, you will not be able to rely on a fee collected regularly even if customers do not use the service.
Ad-based	This is one of the most common models touted by internet startups today, the so-called Facebook model. The service is free, and the revenue comes from click-through or exposure-based advertising. It is great for customers who do not care about busy screens and obtrusive ads. If you are hubristic and like living on the edge, try the early stage "Twitter" model of no revenue, which counts on a critical mass of millions of users potentially being converted into paying customers one day.
Service Add-On	In this model, the product is given away for free and the customers are charged for installation, customization, training, or other services. This is a good model for getting your foot in the door, but be aware that it is basically a services business model with the product as a marketing ("loss leader") cost. The risk is that customers will try to make do with what they can get for free without buying your services and might end up having a sub-par, negative experience because they are untrained or only have access to an intentionally hobbled solution.
Freemium	In this variation on the free model, used by LinkedIn and many others, the basic offering is free, but premium features are available for an additional fee. This also requires a huge investment to get to critical mass, and real work to differentiate and sell premium services to users who are used to paying nothing.
Subscription	The subscription model has been extremely popular because it provides value to both the company and the customer. For customers, the value lies in the convenience: the autopilot simplicity of subscriptions removes the thinking from a purchase decision. Subscribers never have to remember to reorder every month, which gives them the reassurance that they will have whatever they need before they need it. Everything arrives at your door like magic, bypassing the hassle of making a trip to the store or website to place an order. Second, subscriptions offer a flat rate, which helps customers stay within their budget. Last, subscriptions usually bring added value to the customer through bundling or getting many services for the price of one. For businesses, the value of a subscription is the ability to predict revenue through recurring sales and not having to sell the customer on a value proposition and "close a deal" at every transaction. The trick is to make the customers feel as though they are getting recurring value by being subscribers.
Club	Unlike the subscription model, in the club model customers pay recurring fees for the right to purchase a product or, as is often the case, to purchase products at substantially discounted rates. For example, people could pay to be a part of an exclusive dining and travel club that allows members access to sponsored events that nonmembers cannot access. The club model provides a business with steady revenue that is punctuated by customer purchases (e.g., Costco). Use of this model typically signals exclusivity, having access to goods or services that have limited availability or that benefit from a price that has been negotiated on a member's behalf.

8.4 Step 2: Settling on the Right Price

Now that you have a good idea of *how* you are going to charge your customers, you need to figure out *what* you are going to charge them. This is not as easy to discern as you might think. Unlike established businesses, startups create solutions that have never been priced before or that offer value that has not been assessed by large numbers of customers. Because of this lack of certainty affecting a large array of variables, pricing is a big worry for many founders. The alternatives range from giving the product or service away for free, to pricing based on costs, to charging what the market will bear (premium pricing).[1*] The implications of the decision you make are huge, defining your brand image, your funding requirements, and your long-term viability. Recognize that customers are typically wary of overly complex or artificial pricing. Your challenge is to set the right price to match the value of your product or service as perceived by the customer while also providing a healthy return to your business.

Many founders approach pricing as they would a math or accounting problem. They roughly calculate the costs to produce and market the product or service and then add what they think might constitute a fair margin to that number (a variant of the cost-plus method). While product cost is a useful data point to help you figure out what your pricing "floor" might be, it is only a sliver of the information you need to make an informed pricing decision. It is also hard to calculate when you do not have a product yet or some idea of how much offering a service will cost you. Other founders just look at what a potential competitor might be charging for a product and charge a little less to try to get the attention of customers, or a little more to signal to the market that their product is a bit better or more upmarket. Again, information about what competitors are charging for alternatives is very useful, but it is more useful when there are peers in the market producing a solution that is very similar. This is not always the case for startups that are sometimes creating something qualitatively different from what is already out there. Moreover, it is likely that competitors may have priced their solutions incorrectly or priced their solutions for a customer segment you are not targeting. Finally, some people just ask a handful of customers how much they are willing to pay and assume that those on-the-fly reports of willingness to purchase at certain price points provide enough information to discern price. By treating pricing as a math or accounting problem, pricing based on what competitors are charging, or simply asking a handful of potential customers to name their price, you are doing yourself a disservice and forgoing an opportunity to make a stellar decision based on all available sources of data.

Because of these concerns with established pricing methods, I suggest using a simplified variant of the value-based pricing model. This model is largely informed by the

---

*There are many possible pricing strategies available to you that go beyond the scope of this book but that might be helpful if you are struggling to make pricing decisions. These include skimming, matching, undercutting, and many other strategies that may help startups gain footholds in certain markets.

perceptions of potential customers you have already identified and some research into alternative solutions. If unit cost (including production and marketing) calculations are viable for you at this point, you can use that number as a floor for your price. If you cannot generate a believable unit cost estimate at this point, you can integrate that information into your pricing formula later. Here is a simple, four-step sequence you can follow to set a market price:

1. *Focus on a single customer segment.* The first thing to know about value-based pricing is that it always references a beachhead or early-stage target market. A new startup selling very large TVs should focus only on big-screen TV buyers, not on all TV buyers. Entrepreneurs cannot use value-based pricing unless they have an identified a specific beachhead they plan to tackle first. If they are targeting multiple segments (not recommended), they must determine a suitable value-based price for each one, then do their best to come up with an aggregated price that satisfies everyone (a nearly impossible task).

2. *Compare with the next best alternative.* This pricing method works only when the target segment has access to a specific competitor's solution that could be purchased instead. Entrepreneurs engaging in value-based pricing always ask the question, "What would this customer buy if my solution wasn't available?" This "next best alternative" is the essential point of comparison for calculating the value-based price. For solutions that are truly new, without peers, the question the entrepreneur must ask is how much the customer currently spends to tackle the jobs to be done that your solution proposes to address. The "how much" may include a value placed on the customer's time, on different supplies cobbled together to create a solution, or any other cost you can ascertain.

3. *Understand differentiated worth.* The next task is to figure out which features are unique, that is, differentiated from the competitor's offering. In our case, the only differentiated feature of our TV startup is its larger screen size. If the way potential customers in your target market currently solve the problem is costly and/or time-consuming (e.g., commercial-quality projectors), you can try to calculate how much the customer would save by switching to your solution.

4. *Place a dollar amount on the difference between alternatives.* The last step in calculating a value-based price is to estimate the dollar value of the differentiated features. For us, this boils down to: "How much will big-screen TV shoppers pay for an extra five inches of screen size?" and then add that amount (let's say it is $150) to $799, Brand B's price. The value-based price of Brand A's TV is $949. To accomplish this step, marketers typically use qualitative customer interviewing, Asking questions such as "How much do you expect you'll have to pay for this solution?" and "What would a 'just a bit too high' price look like and what would a price that signals 'lack of quality' look like?" Other questions might get at specific feature pricing: "How much more would you be willing to pay to add this feature to the TV you are about to buy?"

Action: Identify a selling price for your product or service. If you are selling it outright, state the retail price. If you are adopting a subscription or club model, note the cost per pay period. Explain why this price makes sense for your solution.

8.5 Step 3: Calculating Market Size

Before a startup can appreciate how much money it might be able to make from a market, it must first understand how much money there is to be made in said market. How big is the pie from which all competitors vying for resources in a market can carve a slice? Just as with pricing, calculating market size can be tricky when there is no active market—that is, when alternatives are not being bought and sold. In that case, market size must be inferred based on reasoned assumptions of what a subset of potential customers might buy in a certain period. The following steps will help you calculate the size of your initial market (see figure 8.1):

1. Start by determining your *total addressable market (TAM)*. The TAM represents the total number of people you think might conceivably use your solution. Think of it as the total number of people you would market to if you were a larger company with a big budget. There are two methods people typically use to calculate TAM. The first is known as the bottom-up method—it requires you to figure out how many people exist within market by combining insights from lists you obtain from potential channel partners, your own landing page, industry association groups, and so on. If you already have some traction with customers, feel free to use your own, grounded data to aid in this calculation. For instance, to calculate the TAM for a local craft brewery using a bottom-up method, a founding team might rely on counting taps in a geographic area. The data can then be used to extrapolate how many taps there might be across broader geographic areas. Eventually, you might have a good guess as to how many taps there are in North American Urban Areas and how many dollars each tap makes in a certain period (e.g., a year). Founding teams also use more top-down methods such as marketing databases and census figures to double-check on their more organically derived estimate. When you build your startup's forecast, it might

FIGURE 8.1
Market Sizing Layers.

be advisable to combine both the bottom-up and top-down methods, especially if you plan to achieve a strong growth curve by means of external funding. One tactic that is increasingly popular is to use the bottom-up method for your short-term forecast (one to two years ahead) and the top-down method for the longer term (three to five years ahead). Doing so enables you to substantiate and defend your short-term targets very well, and bringing in your long-term targets indicates your desired market share and shows investors the scale of your ambition.

2. Next, try to identify the portion of the TAM that, given your limited resources and geographic and operational constraints, you can serve. This is called your *serviceable available market (SAM)*. Calculating SAM is particularly relevant to businesses that are faced with material constraints and that, unlike an app-based business, cannot sell to anyone without incurring additional costs. If we think of our brewery again, we might consider that a serviceable market will be limited by how many kegs and beer cans our facilities can produce, as well as by the geographic constraints of the distributors with which we plan to contract.

3. The last number you need to calculate to create your market size estimate is a subset of the SAM. The *beachhead market* is representative of the customers you plan to market to in the first twenty-four months of your business's existence. Why only twenty-four months? The customers served in the early months are in your first and perhaps your second or third persona categories. The beachhead is therefore equal to your sales target, as it represents the value of the market share you aim to capture, given existing competitors and competitors that might enter the market within that short period. Your marketing will target those customers first and, most likely, exclusively. This subset comprises

the people you are committed to impressing with the first iteration of your product or service and who will become evangelists for your brand as you expand.

Action: Calculate your TAM, SAM, and beachhead market using both top-down and bottom-up data sources. When estimating these variables, aim for profitability within a reasonable time frame (typically twenty-four months). In other words, at some point all costs and expenses should not exceed your revenue targets anymore, so that you get to a positive EBITDA (earnings before interest, taxes, depreciation, and amortization). Detail your calculation and list all data sources used below:

8.6   Step 4: Projecting Sales Revenue

Entrepreneurs can't forecast accurately because they are trying something fundamentally new. So, they will often be laughably behind plan—and on the brink of success.
—Eric Ries, author of *The Lean Startup*

Although some investors may be enticed by the potential of a fast-growing market with few rivals, most angel funds and venture capitalists will expect founders, even those who haven't sold anything yet, to describe how they will approach capturing a target market. This will require the founder to outline a go-to-market plan and describe how leads captured in executing that plan will be converted into cash flow for the company. The creation of a go-to-market plan, which may include the use of various marketing channels and campaigns, is beyond the scope of this chapter, but an estimate of the leads to be derived from that plan is a necessary component of early-stage revenue projection.

To complete the following steps, please refer to the companion MS Excel workbook. I have designed it to support the procedures that follow and provide you with information you will need to craft a rudimentary, early-stage financial projection. Note that in the "Revenue Projection" tab of the workbook, the first cell asks you to input the size of your total addressable market (TAM), along with the expected growth rate for that market in the subsequent twenty-four months. Once these figures are entered, the formulas will auto-populate the remaining cells in that row. As with all other calculations, founders should adjust numbers as more complete information becomes available. Like the BMC, the financial projection workbook should be treated as a living document that is adjusted as often as new findings about the business and its external environment come to light.

Next, founders should think carefully how many **leads**[†] they expect to generate each month. For instance, if the target market for Giant Screen TVs is about ten million potential buyers, and a business thinks it can generate about one thousand leads per month using marketing campaigns outlined in the go-to-market plan, the founder would put 1,000 in the "Leads" row. If the founder expects that the number of leads generated will grow by 10 percent per month, they will enter 10% in the next row.

A **sale** is the result of a converted lead. So, to calculate estimated sales volume, a founder might first begin by hypothesizing a conversion rate. In short, out of those one thousand leads, how many do I think I can convert into paying customers? If I expect that I can convert 5 percent of those customers, I will have about fifty sales per month. If the average price of a gigantic flat screen TV is $15,000, I will bring in $750,000 in sales.

Here we have made a series of assumptions that are based on reasoned estimates of three variables: market size, lead generation, and conversion rate. Each of these assumptions should be based on the best data you can find and that you, as you think about approaching investors, would feel comfortable defending. The first step, however, is to make best guesses and go through the process of projecting so that you are aware of all the numbers that are still relatively fuzzy. As you progress, you will learn about seasonality, channel idiosyncrasies, and other inputs that will influence your revenue projections. The key is to incorporate these into your projections slowly as you build increased confidence in your numbers.

Action: Complete the "Revenue Projection" tab in the financial projection Excel workbook to the best of your ability. Refer to the comments provided in certain cells to guide you as you enter your best guesses.

8.7 Step 5: Projecting Expenses

The key activities and key resources buildings blocks of the BMC can be your starting point for understanding the cost drivers of your venture. Performing key activities that

---

[†]Lead generation is critical to the sustained success and growth of all businesses. Typically, generating leads is the first step in the sales process. The easiest way to understand the term is to think of a lead as the start of the journey. A lead is someone who may be interested in a product or service that you provide, but you have no context as to what or why. The main difference between a lead and a prospect is that your lead has moved beyond one-way communication and has now engaged with you. Such two-way communication suggests that the lead has real potential to buy from your business. This is when the lead becomes a sales prospect.

support your value propositions will cost your venture. Purchasing or gaining access to key resources (e.g., human capital, intellectual property) also generates expenses that, along with the activities, become part of the venture cost structure.

Prelaunch Expenses   Every startup will have to contend with three types of costs: those required to get a business off the ground and two types of recurring costs that are incurred thereafter: fixed costs (which are incurred whether or not a sale is made) and variable costs (which are incurred when a sale is made). Prelaunch costs might include the costs of software development, construction, equipment purchases, and other expenses that need to be incurred right away to get the business going before the doors open or the first download is made from the app store. In the Excel addendum, you will notice a tab ("Prelaunch Expenses") that includes about a dozen expenses that are typically incurred by businesses being founded. Note that this estimate assumes that you do not already have assets you can leverage to reduce initial expenses. If you do, be sure to account for those manually.

Action: Complete the "Prelaunch Expenses" tab in the financial projection Excel worksheet to the best of your ability.

Operating Expenses   Operating expenses are those pesky costs that are incurred month in and month out. They range from the rent check you owe your landlord for your office space to the cost of the glossy brochures your salespeople asked for so that they could impress potential customers. Many startups fail to plan carefully for mundane costs such as subscriptions to software packages, bank fees, server space dues, utility payments, and the like. The list goes on and on. However, having a good sense of what these expenses might be will often help you ask investors for just the money you need and prevent needless stress.

Action: Complete the "Operating Expenses" tab in the financial projection Excel worksheet to the best of your ability.

Salary Expenses   Payroll costs tend to be among the largest for any startup, particularly those that sell their solution through a sales team. While they are technically expenses related to operating a venture, by separating out payroll you can get a better sense of how much your value proposition is human-powered. Having the right mix of people and paying the right salary to employees is a struggle for any first-time CEO. Waiting too long to hire a salesperson may depress your revenue curve significantly and make it seem as though your value proposition is not resonating. Hiring someone too soon may mean that person becomes a drain on resources that does not yield positive outcomes that outweigh expenses.

Action: Complete the "Salary Expenses" tab in the financial projection Excel worksheet to the best of your ability.

8.8   Route Monitoring: Completing Your Financial Projection

Once all tabs are properly completed in the workbook, you will have completed your first, rudimentary financial projection. In its current state, this projection has flaws. The document will become more valuable as you tweak numbers and continue to add better estimates. It is, nevertheless, very valuable—even in its current state—to investors who are trying to assess your thought process and verify that your assumptions are well researched.[2] Part of how investors assess your idea is by scrutinizing a projected income statement (look for the tab in your workbook), otherwise known as a profit-and-loss (P&L) projection. Your P&L offers investors a view of your business that they can contrast with other opportunities.

Please make note of all the graphs generated through your inputs, and step into the investors' shoes. Does how the projection is laid out suggest that you, the founder, will be a good steward of investors' money? Is the outlook bright, or are there some red flags that might be reasons for one not to invest? Investors can use a break-even analysis to determine when your business will start making more money than it has taken in, an important milestone that evades many entrepreneurs. It is expected that a business will be operating in the red for months or even years, but recovery and high growth must be in the cards. If not, you will have to go back to the drawing board and reconsider your business model!

Finally, use the "Metrics" tab in the workbook to examine how well your business is performing across some of the key numbers experienced investors care about. These include the following:

- The *lead conversion rate* measures the percentage of your leads that end up being converted to opportunities every month. To calculate lead conversion rate, divide the number of leads converted to opportunities in a period by the number of leads created in that period.

- *Customer churn* is the percentage of customers who stopped using your company's product or service during a certain time frame. You can calculate churn rate by dividing the number of customers you lost during that time—say, a month—by the number of customers you had at the beginning of that period. For example, if you start your month with 400 customers and end with 380, your churn rate is 5 percent because you lost 5 percent (20) of your customers. This metric is particularly important to businesses that adopt a subscription or club revenue model.

- *Customer acquisition cost* (CAC) is the cost associated with convincing a customer to buy a solution, that is, the total sales and marketing costs required to earn a new customer over a specific period. This metric plays a major role in calculating the value of the customer to the company and the resulting return on investment (ROI) of acquisition.[3] It helps a founder decide how much can be profitably spent on a customer and how much is too much. To compute the cost to acquire a customer, CAC, you would take your entire cost of sales and marketing over a given period, including salaries and other head-count-related expenses, and divide it by the number of customers that you acquired in that period. (In pure software or web-based businesses where the head count does not need to grow as customer acquisition scales up, it is also very useful to look at customer acquisition costs without the head count costs.)[4]

- *Customer lifetime value* (CLV, often CLTV), lifetime customer value (LCV), or lifetime value (LTV) is a prediction of the net profit that can attributed to the entire future relationship with a customer. How much can the founders capture from a customer before the customer terminates the relationship? The prediction model can have varying levels of sophistication and accuracy, ranging from a crude heuristic to the use of complex predictive analytics techniques. CLV is an important concept in that it encourages firms to shift their focus from quarterly profits to the long-term health of their customer relationships. To compute the LTV of a customer relationship, you look at the gross margin that you expect to make from that customer over the lifetime of your relationship. Gross margin should take into consideration any support, installation, and servicing costs.

8.9   Destination: Reflection and Next Steps

As you work either to bootstrap your business or take in money from investors, your financials will grow increasingly complex. When you begin hawking your solution, invoicing, taxation, and other minutiae will grow into an increasingly onerous part of your job. Many founders decide that hiring an accountant or perhaps a freelance financial officer makes sense once dealing with these requirements starts to get in the way of time that might otherwise be devoted to making sales, developing partnerships, and engaging in other higher-priority activities that cannot be outsourced. In preparation for that day, I suggest you begin looking into the following:

- Build a relationship with an independent accountant or accounting firm that comes recommended by other founders and that has experience dealing with early-stage firms. If possible, reach out to accountants who have experience in the industry you are entering; they may become important sources of advice.

- Be ready to transition from the Excel spreadsheet you have put together to a proprietary accounting program (e.g., Quickbooks) that will make calculating taxes and invoicing more seamless. Consult your accountant regarding which program is appropriate for your business.

- Decide how and when you will share financial data. This decision should involve and pertain to all members of the founding team privy to the information. Use this discussion as an opportunity to have a broader discussion about data privacy and sharing.

- Consult the resource page on the MIT Press website (https://mitpress.mit.edu/massa -wild). Content related to this chapter can be found under Founder Resources/Chapter 8.

9 Pitching Your Startup

Objectives

- Create a pitch slide deck that impresses across all the major elements that investors and competition judges care about.
- Deploy various techniques to ensure the appeal and cohesiveness of your pitch deck.
- Practice delivering your pitch to different audiences and creating variations that fit different situations.

9.1 Mini Case: Pitching RentCheck

Lydia Winkler and Marco Nelson had some harrowing firsthand experiences in the residential rental property market. Lydia was working on a law degree and an MBA at Tulane University while suing a former landlord who refused to return her security deposit. Marco, Lydia's classmate in the MBA program, owned properties in and out of state. He was familiar with how murky and complicated the property inspection process can get, especially if one is going to school full-time and working with tenants hundreds of miles away. Marco heard about Lydia's lawsuit during orientation and started a conversation. The two commiserated over their shared frustrations and decided to start investigating potential solutions. As Lydia notes, "We were on a mission to make the rental market more just." Soon they found themselves using class projects in different subject areas to shape different building blocks in their business model.

The many conversations with landlords and renters that followed yielded valuable insights and lots of horror stories featuring shady activities by unethical landlords and destructive behaviors by renters. They found that, despite the constant threat of lawsuits and conflict, most independent landlords relied on informal systems to keep track of move-ins and move-outs. They were often overwhelmed by paperwork and in a rush to keep properties occupied. According to Marco, the startup's "biggest competitor was still pen and paper" and the biggest challenge was to convince landlords to adopt anything technological. Their data told them that the key was to put together a secure, transparent solution that would address the concerns of worried renters and solve real problems being experienced by overwhelmed landlords.

The result of Lydia and Marco's combined experience, ingenuity, and many hours of customer validation interviews and developer meetings was RentCheck, an app that allows renters and landlords to complete a standardized, frictionless rental inspection using smart-phones. RentCheck users—both landlords and renters—can track the condition of a property using time-stamped photos and access inspection records at any time. It gives renters a record of what the property looked like when they moved in and gives landlords the peace of mind that tenants will move in seamlessly and not destroy the property. Both parties benefit from a convenient, secure, transparent way to complete property inspections. Early traction numbers provided further support for the founding team's hypotheses: RentCheck was signing up both renters and landlords, particularly landlords struggling to manage multiple properties, much more quickly than they expected.

Yet, despite a promising revenue model and a go-to-market plan that was already showing traction, the team was worried that investors would be turned off by the fact that RentCheck was yet another financial technology app. The money they needed to raise to expand their footprint and capitalize on early traction would depend on their ability to make a compelling pitch in a market crowded with **fintech*** solutions. So they decided to work hard on their pitch. They recruited faculty, received lots of coaching, and applied to several pitch competitions: "In the months that followed graduation, we pitched in seven or eight pitch competitions and brought in over $100,000 in prize money." The pair also booked a trip to Silicon Valley to pitch to people who were seeing some of the best **deal flow**† in the country. They wanted to hone their pitch deck and test their skills in the most cutthroat environment they could find and learn as quickly as possible: "The more you pitch, the more questions you are fielding—we incorporated all of that experience into the deck so that we could address concerns before they were raised."

By the end of this grueling process, their go-to pitch deck contained all essential elements organized in a way that built both excitement and trust. The result was several meetings with investors who, before seeing the RentCheck team present, had seldom considered investing in app-based startups and were now ready be part of a seed round.

---

*Fintech is a term used in the investment community to refer to innovations in the financial and technology crossover space, and typically refers to companies or services that use technology to provide financial services to businesses or consumers.

†Deal flow is a term used by venture capitalists, angel investors, private equity investors, and investment bankers to refer to the rate at which they receive requests for investment, or "asks."

9.2   Orientation: Pitching Your Startup

A pitch is a persuasive speech intended to elicit a response from an audience. As a startup founder, you will be pitching a lot. You will pitch to recruit founding team members, to impress judges at pitch competitions, and to inform and attract funders, such as friends and family, equity investors, and bank loan officers. Being the head of an organization that is still seeking **legitimacy**[1] means you will have to work hard to convince all of these audiences not only that your idea is worth attending to[‡] but that you are the right person to launch the venture that executes the idea.[2]

In this chapter, we focus on the most structured and, most likely, the highest-stakes pitch you will be making on a regular basis—the short-form investor pitch. This form of pitch tends to last between seven and twenty minutes and is designed to provide an audience of investors with an overview of your proposed business. At the end of the pitch is an ask for money, mentorship, and/or technical and professional assistance. After creating this version of the pitch, you will have a base deck that you can expand on for longer investor meetings, reframe for internal presentations to employees, or shorten for lightning pitch competitions. The good news is that the work you have done thus far by completing the exercises in this book will provide you with the content you need to complete the deck. All you need do is design a pitch deck that is as cohesive and compelling to your intended audience as possible.

Before I jump into providing you with slide-by-slide advice and a sample deck, I will offer some advice that I follow myself and that has helped many of my colleagues and students win pitch competitions:

- Keep slide **formatting** as straightforward and professional as possible. I often see well-intentioned founders create slides that are difficult to read or are cluttered with unnecessary elements, such as clip art or photos, that do not help make a case for investment. To keep this from happening to you, I suggest you follow a few rules of thumb that are easy to implement once you put yourself into the shoes of your audience. Make sure people can read the name of your business from twenty feet away (at least 32-point font size). The fonts and graphic standards (e.g., colors) used in your slides should flow through to the rest of the presentation so that there is no jarring effect as you move between slides. It is fine to use design elements such as icons and graphics but keep them cohesive and use them sparingly. Do not use slide templates or designs provided by PowerPoint or Keynote because it is likely that audience members have seen them and used them many times. Remember, you are probably pitching to people who have pitched a business idea or two themselves. The impression left by

---

[‡]Because many startups lack any sort of operating history, they are burdened by high uncertainty about their viability. This may mean that investors, experts, and other key stakeholders may be reluctant to invest time and treasure at an early stage. The work of the founder during the pre-seed and seed stages is to overcome this "liability of newness" and engender confidence. Founders can do so in several ways, such as by conveying personal, domain-related credibility and communicating the high quality of relationships with other stakeholders.

these template designs is that you are too lazy to craft your own design or invest time in making yourself appear professional. If you are not technically savvy and insist on using templates, consider less popular third-party slide templates (e.g., Canva).

- The **slide order** I lay out here is only a boilerplate and should not be followed blindly. Some ideas may benefit from changes in slide order; some slides may need to be excluded for open audiences and included when you are presenting to a smaller group of investors. Ultimately, it is up to you to decide the best way to present your business. When in doubt, ask questions and get feedback from people who have pitched successfully before.

- **Presentation order** matters when it comes to pitch competitions or even pitches to investors. Your audience will likely be listening to other pitches before or after yours. Researchers disagree whether going first or going last is ideal, for a variety of reasons. Several studies argue that entrepreneurs would likely be better off pitching early because audiences pay more attention to what they see first,[3] because judges of all sorts tend to become harsher over time,[4] or because judges **satisfice**,[5][§] settling on the first tolerable option. Other studies suggest that entrepreneurs would be better off pitching late because evaluators recall and make decisions based on recent information or because judges find it difficult initially to calibrate performance and are thus too harsh in the beginning.[6] The only option that scholars across the board agree is not ideal is to occupy the middle. So, if you have any influence over the order in which you will present, try to go first or last.

- The **presenter** is the most important element of the presentation. If you have the perfect slide deck and your presenter is not up to the task of convincingly delivering the content, your ideas will not resonate. Moreover, researcher have shown that conveying passion has a real impact on the likelihood that a pitch will attract funding.[7][¶] It is advisable that the founder or the CEO of the venture take the stage and pitch—it is what investors expect, and doing otherwise may raise some eyebrows. If the founder is abysmal at public speaking, you have a few options: (1) You can limit the role of the founder by having them bookend the pitch by introducing the venture and ending the presentation. In this case, another member of the founding team can fill in the gap. (2) You can also change the nature of the presentation to be a better fit for the founder. More introverted or technical founders sometimes do not deliver a stage show but instead take a more informal, conversational tone when presenting.[8][**] One

---

[§] The term *satisficing*, a portmanteau of satisfy and suffice, was made popular by Herbert A. Simon in 1955. Simon used the satisficing construct to explain the behavior of decision makers when an optimal solution cannot be determined. In these situations, people tend to settle for the first acceptable alternative even if it is not ideal. Herbert A. Simon, "A Behavioral Model of Rational Choice," *The Quarterly Journal of Economics* 69, no. 1 (1955): 99–118.

[¶] Founders displaying high passion increase investor neural engagement by 39 percent and investor interest in the venture by 26 percent over those displaying low passion.

[**] Extant research shows that investors use sets of stereotypes—"person prototypes"—to categorize people pitching ideas in the first moments of interaction. This instant typecasting can be a disadvantage, but if a pitcher fits

crucial thing to avoid is crowding a stage or conference room with too many members of the founding team. People who do not have a clear role should be in the audience and not standing around on stage.

- It may seem silly, but major pitches can be sunk by seemingly small **technology** issues, ranging from faulty clickers to undone slide formatting. The key is to test your deck before the presentation, have it in different formats, and keep open lines of communication with people hosting pitch competitions or investor meetings. Never pitch before you have seen your deck and demo working as intended.

9.3   Step 1: Setting the Stage

Slide 1: The Intro: The first slide in your deck will likely be on screen for a while as your audience settles, as technical difficulties are addressed, and as you introduce yourself and your idea. The *goal* of this slide is to set the tone for the entire pitch and to give your audience a preview of what your business is all about. Consider that, in many cases, your audience will be hearing several pitches in sequence, meaning they need to refocus and reset their expectations several times over. They may also be taking notes on your presentation and will need to know the name of your company. Be conscious, therefore, of what you are projecting. Keep your tone and energy positive but not manic or inauthentic. Stand tall and speak confidently even before you officially start your pitch: you are looking forward to blowing the audience away with a great idea that has been validated thoroughly. Never read what you are saying—remember that you are also selling yourself as a future CEO. CEOs do not read pitches from notecards or read their slides in a monotone. You may be telling yourself that you are not a gifted speaker. I urge you to think about delivering this speech as any other skill that requires practice and dedication.

There are three *key components* that are standard for a pitch introduction slide: (1) the name of your organization, featured in large type or integrated into an easy-to-read logo; (2) a branded email address (e.g., info@lemonation.com) so that interested investors or audience members with questions can follow up; and (3) a URL that links to a landing page designed to collect email addresses or social media credentials from audience members. Some pitches contain *extra components* designed to enhance understanding of the slide or to make it easier for audience members to maintain contact with the business. These are (1) a slogan that elaborates on or clarifies what the company does, (2) social media links designed to encourage audience member exploration, and (3) a notice that the slide deck you are presenting is confidential or restricted and should not be distributed. I advise you to use these components and any additional graphics sparingly (if at all) as they can make a title slide look cluttered. Simplicity should be your mantra here, as you want attention to be on you and not on the slides.

_____

an investor's idea of what a "technical founder" should look and sound like, they may get away with being less than polished or convincing. Pitchers may therefore attempt to play to a stereotype and see their ideas resonate.

FIGURE 9.1
Title Slide.

The first slide in the "Syllaber" slide deck shown in figure 9.1 follows this advice and errs on the side of minimalism. I will use slides from this deck to illustrate pointers I give in the rest of this chapter. Please note that the Syllaber deck represents one possible way for you to structure your presentation and should not be considered the only way to do it. Every venture should be pitched in a way that tells its amazing story clearly and authentically and not in a way that perfectly fits a contrived template.

Most founders will kick off their pitch by introducing themselves briefly (e.g., "I'm Elon Musk") and their business (e.g., "and I'm a cofounder of Tesla, an auto company that will launch an all-electric future"). Some founders take the extra step of thanking their audience and expressing how pleased they are to have the opportunity to present their ideas. When presentation norms are not set by organizers, speakers may also give audience members a sense of how long their pitch will take and whether they plan to take questions during or after the pitch.

Slide 2: Founding Team/Advisers: The second slide in your deck (figure 9.2) is your first opportunity to introduce a founding team and give a nod to any advisers or board members who have publicly committed to supporting your venture. The introduction of both stakeholder groups is an important opportunity to showcase the talent and experience that will be working on your venture at launch. After the first impression you create with the introductory slide, the second slide functions to anchor your audience. By anchoring I mean you establish in their mind the conception that your team is qualified and that you have the support of well-connected, knowledgeable experts.[9][††] Doing so will make the potential success story you are about to sell much more believable.[10]

[††] Psychologists have found that people tend to heavily favor the first piece of information they learn about a person or, in this case, a startup. This anchoring bias or anchoring effect can have significantly more influence on an audience member's perceptions than information they receive in the middle of a pitch.

Felipe Massa, Ph.D.
Founder and C.E.O.

Business Professor
Advised over 5,000 startups

Dax Rodriguez
Technology

Former programmer for
leading LMS company
Award-winning Experience
Designer

Allegra Robertson
Sales

Former textbook sales
manager
More than $3 million in
academic sales over 2 years

FIGURE 9.2
Team Slide.

The *key components* of this slide include (1) high-resolution, professional photographs of founding team members who have a well-balanced set of qualifications; (2) brief descriptions (typically photo captions) that include the names of the founding team members, their roles, and their qualifications (the roles described here should not be too specific, such as director of marketing, because founding team members are expected to work across functional areas as the business gets under way. It is important, however, for the descriptions to convey that the pieces necessary to launch this venture are in place. Focus on startup experience if possible); and (3) a list of advisors, which lends gravitas to the startup and signals connections to important investor and expert communities. The Syllaber example shown in figure 9.2 uses made-up credentials and team members to illustrate the types of experience an investor may be looking for when examining a founding team. Notice that the focus is on relevant domain and startup experience.

Importantly, if the qualifications you have available to present are not stellar (e.g., no experience or no relevant expertise), you might want to move the team slide to the back of the pitch deck. After all, you do not want to anchor your audience on the fact that your team is inexperienced or unqualified to deliver on the promises you are about to make. By placing the slide at or near the end of the deck, you will have time to use your presentation skills, great ideas, and validation to get audience members so excited that they may pay little attention your lackluster or unrelated experience.

9.4   Step 2: Establishing the Problem

Slide 3: The Problem/Job to Be Done: The job to be done or problem slide is self-explanatory, particularly after the work you have done to carefully define what you are tackling for your customers. Your goal is to draw in the audience by presenting a shocking statistic, telling a compelling story that puts the problem in focus, or using some form of creative data display. I suggest focusing on a primary data point that clearly and concisely illustrates the pain point for a specific customer segment. Do not try to create a laundry list of problems—go with your strongest reason for starting the business (figures 9.3 and 9.4).

The *key components* of the problem slide include (1) a statement that concisely describes the problem or job to be done to a lay audience, and (2) a clear reason why solving this problem is important to a specific customer segment (a tier 1 problem, a need, a pain point). Some founders choose to make their narrative thread richer and easier to follow by introducing a persona that will be used throughout the pitch. The persona may, for instance, be the customer experiencing the problem or desperately keen on tackling the job to be done. Some also try to explain why no one has tried to tackle the problem before as a setup for upcoming slides designed to convince audiences that this team is in possession of the "special sauce" needed to finally tackle the problem at hand.

Problem slides are foundational. If the problem is not believable or seems unimportant to your audience, whatever you say next will be undermined. I decided to split my problem slide into two for Syllaber so that I could frame the context first and then dig a bit deeper into what transpires to trigger a pain point for my core customer: the college instructor seen working at his desk.

"Most instructors spend at least two hours in prep time outside class for every hour spent inside class."

—American Faculty Association

FIGURE 9.3
Problem Slide 1.

All that effort is undermined by...

- Unforeseen events that lead to course interruptions
- Student work ethic issues that impede course progression
- Miscommunications between student and instructor
- Overscheduling, which overwhelms instructors and leads to decreased course quality

FIGURE 9.4
Problem Slide 2.

Slide 4: Problem Validation: After proposing your problem and persona in the first few chapters of this book, you were asked to "get out of the building" and conduct interviews with potential customers to determine if the job you sought to tackle rang top-of-mind and urgent. The *goal* of this slide is to buttress the problem statement in the previous slide with evidence. This evidence can come in the form of direct quotations from your interviews or from other sources of data such as industry reports or empirical studies. As with any of the slides you use in your pitch, use the space you have wisely and showcase only your most incontrovertible evidence.

The *key components* of the problem validation slide (figures 9.5 and 9.6) include (1) evidence of the presence and urgency of the job to be done or problem you are tackling with your solution and (2) short descriptions of your sources to demonstrate that they cohere with the persona you proposed. Some founders choose to use this slide as an opportunity to introduce the audience to a persona that they will thread through the rest of the presentation. I use two sources of data in the examples I provide in this section: opportunity validation interviews with twenty-two college instructors in targeted departments and a survey conducted through my landing page. Together they provide solid backing to the severity and urgency of the issue I am tackling.

9.5   Step 3: Showcasing Your Solution

Slide 5: Solution: Now that you have laid the groundwork by establishing the existence and urgency of your job to be done, you can turn your attention to the core of your presentation:

n = 22 college instructors in Business, Engineering, and Design

Dept. Chair,
Professor, Design

I consider myself a patient person, but having to manually change all the dates on my syllabus every time a class gets canceled or I must extend a lecture to another day really irks me.

Ph.D. Candidate,
Management

I just got my first academic job last month and found out that they use a different LMS I'm not familiar with... All the prep I did not Canvas is pretty much useless.

Asst. Professor,
Corporate Social
Responsibility

It's not just a time suck, it's off-putting to print out 50 copies of a twelve-page syllabus every time I teach a social responsibility class designed to make the students better stewards of the environment.

Adjunct Professor,
Engineering

I have teaching appointments in three different places, but I use the same stuff. It's a pain to have to rebrand everything and to adjust to different class lengths.

FIGURE 9.5
Problem Validation Slide 1.

Survey:
n = 280 college instructors sourced from launch page/company Facebook profile

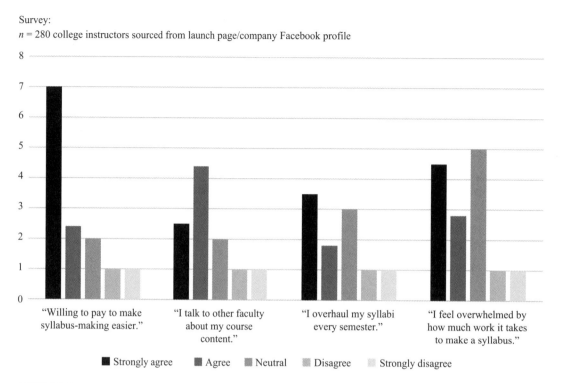

FIGURE 9.6
Problem Validation Slide 2.

the solution. As the term implies, a solution should fully address the problem you have posed. If the problem is too large or too complex, it is unlikely that a single startup's solution will be able to fully resolve it. Therefore, it is important that your problem statement does not exceed the scope of your solution. At the same time, the solution should not be excessively complex or claim to be a panacea that may prove impossible to build or implement. Investors are looking for a healthy balance of ambition and pragmatism.

The *key components* of the solution slide (figure 9.7) typically include (1) one punchy sentence nailing the essence of what your solution is and does (Is it a web application or a device? Is it a franchise or a single store?), as well as how it tackles the problem in a way that makes sense, and (2) a brief list of top-line features that you need to highlight to capture how the problem is tackled and the value proposition attached to the features (Is it convenient? Easy to use? Beautifully designed?). In the example provided, I offer a top-line description of what my solution is and a set of three broad features that support that description. It is easy to overload audiences with text and talk when describing your solution or its key features, so conciseness should be at the top of your mind.

Slide 6: Demo/Customer Use Case: Now that you have told your audience what your solution is, it is time to showcase it in a positive light. There are many ways to show rather

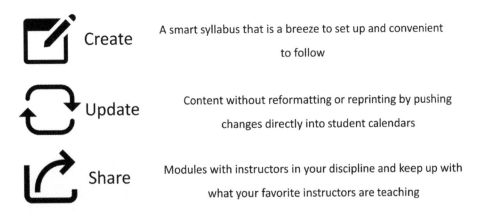

SYLLABER is an easy-to-use web-based application

Create — A smart syllabus that is a breeze to set up and convenient to follow

Update — Content without reformatting or reprinting by pushing changes directly into student calendars

Share — Modules with instructors in your discipline and keep up with what your favorite instructors are teaching

FIGURE 9.7
Solution Slide.

than tell people about your solution. Some founders favor static demos such as device schematics, photographs of a prototype, or floor plans for a store. The most compelling demos are, in my opinion, dynamic representations of a great customer experience. Good demos focus on how a tangible solution overcomes problems that are truly important to the customer. Bad demos go through feature after feature in excruciating detail without connecting to results that matter. Instead of showing screenshots of your web application, tell a story from a customer's perspective. It might be a snapshot in time of how that customer went from experiencing a problem to using your solution to resolve the problem. Instead of showing a store layout, show a video of a customer interacting with friendly staff or reliable technology to tackle their problem. The point is to make the audience members feel as though they were in the shoes of the customer. Once they are immersed, you wow them with what is great about your solution.

The *key component* of the demo slide (figure 9.8) (or, more likely, a set of slides, a video, or a physical prototype) is a simple, well-structured narrative. Some choose to use their persona to anchor this narrative with a character who is now familiar to the audience. In the Syllaber example we see an instructor creating a class on the Syllaber web application and wowing a student. Note that I do not include all the features I could or focus too deeply on a single element. I could also break up this slide into multiple slides so that each stage in the use case or each screen in the web app is clearly distinguishable by the audience. It is up to you to decide what platform works best to show off your innovation.

Slide 7: Solution Validation: Just as the problem validation slide provided evidence of the problem, the solution validation slide provides evidence that the solution impressed

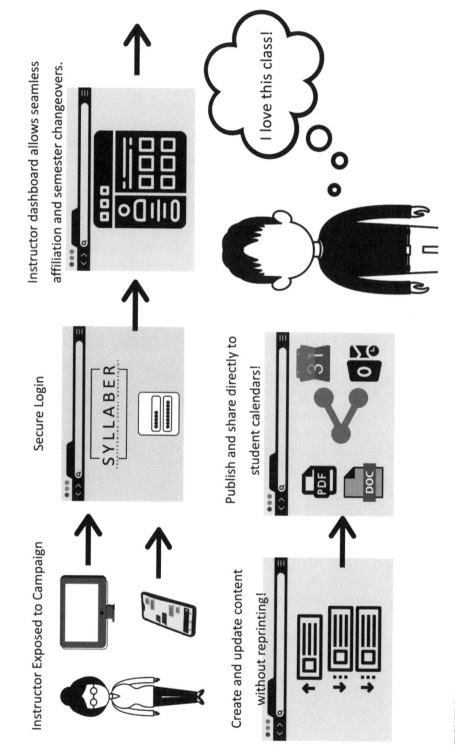

FIGURE 9.8
Demo Slide.

potential customers and did a great job of tackling a problem. Several types of evidence can be marshaled as solution validation, including data from interviews, surveys, A/B tests, and social media reactions. Because of this abundance of options, solution validation is often covered in more than a single slide. However, even though you may have a lot of different data to display, it is important to show only your strongest evidence and leave additional evidence in your back pocket (or in hidden slides) in case you sense doubt from the audience.

The *key component* of the solution validation slide (figure 9.9.) is curated evidence that demonstrates not just tepid interest in the solution but genuine excitement on the part of customers who fit a targeted persona profile. In the example I provide, you can see real enthusiasm from instructors across the business, engineering, and design disciplines I targeted. Their comments read a lot like testimonials and emphasize an emotional connection to the solution or to the experience of having a job to be done tackled in a better way.

9.6   Step 4: Capturing Opportunity

Slide 8: Revenue Model: The revenue model slide should convey to the audience how you plan on charging customers as well as why this model is appropriate. If it is a key differentiator for your business, it may also be beneficial to contrast your revenue model with those of your competitors.

The *key components* of the revenue model slide (figure 9.10) include (1) the type of revenue model you have chosen (e.g., leasing, subscription), and (2) information on how much in actual currency you plan to charge. The more revenue streams you require to support your business, the more complicated this slide may become. So, consider the value of a straightforward revenue model both in investor presentations and in selling to customers who might get frustrated by pricing that is difficult to understand. In the example, I provide information on a two-tiered pricing structure, one for individual instructors and another for higher-volume institutional clients such as universities. I also tout a commitment to give away the product to verified student teachers. This may seem like kindness at first, but it is really a good way to build usage habits in a population that will soon become my principal target.

Slide 9: Market Opportunity: You have now shown that people who match your persona profile are very interested in your solution. For this interest to be considered a legitimate business opportunity, a large enough market must be willing to buy your solution. In this slide you will quantify the market you are targeting.

The *key components* of the market opportunity slide (figure 9.11) include (1) a figure that demonstrates the size and revenue potential (roughly, size multiplied by the price you intend to charge for your solution) of your beachhead, serviceable available market (SAM) and total addressable market (TAM), and (2) the expected growth rate

n = 38 college instructors in Business, Engineering, and Design

I love the fact that I have the option of printing my syllabus or sharing it directly via my students' calendars. They didn't even have to log on to Blackboard to get their assignments.

Asst. Professor, Finance

They cancel classes where I teach for weather all the time. I think my favorite feature is the live update tab —I can just move classes around by dragging and dropping. I didn't have to retype anything!

Adjunct Professor, Engineering

I thought transitioning to Syllaber would take a lot of time, but the official calendar from my school was already there when I clicked through! It was convenient and took me a lot less time!

Dept. Chair, Professor, Design

I'm not usually an early adopter, but I wanted to share my content with assistant professors and adjuncts in my department. Syllaber made sharing all of it a lot easier!

Professor, Entrepreneurship

FIGURE 9.9
Solution Validation Slide.

Subscription Revenue Model: Charge a monthly use fee or a discounted annual fee

Price of $11.95/month ($120/year), discounted by 15% for institutions with over 100 users

Free to verified student teachers enrolled in graduate programs for 2 years

FIGURE 9.10
Revenue Model Slide.

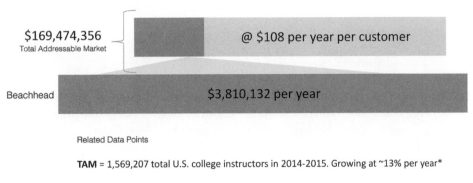

$169,474,356
Total Addressable Market

@ $108 per year per customer

Beachhead

$3,810,132 per year

Related Data Points

TAM = 1,569,207 total U.S. college instructors in 2014-2015. Growing at ~13% per year*

Beachhead = 35,279 AACSB business school faculty**

FIGURE 9.11
Market Opportunity Slide. Sources: * US Bureau of Statistics. ** AACSB International.

of this market. Many presenters will show TAM/SAM/beachhead in a figure and use it to explain how and why they parsed the market in that way. In the example, I try to capture my explanation of market opportunity graphically. I show that the beachhead I aim to capture constitutes only a small chunk of a much richer and more lucrative opportunity.

Slide 10: Competitive Landscape: This slide is a good opportunity for you to convey to your audience that you have considered not only who your direct competitors or alternative solutions might be but also that you are well positioned to displace them. You might also want to convey why and how they are not a compelling threat to your business. Mention key differentiators: How are you uniquely positioned for success? If you have real, direct competitors, make sure you go a little deeper to explain how and you will challenge their market position, and why. If you are planning to work with incumbents by feeding into their value chains, explain that strategy here.

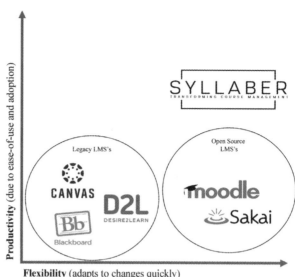

FIGURE 9.12
Competition Slide.

The *key components* of a competitive landscape analysis (figure 9.12) include (1) a perceptual map showing how you relate to others present in a particular market and how you beat them across value propositions that matter to a beachhead, and (2) a feature comparison chart that highlights what features or "special sauce" distinguish you from incumbents. Depending on how compelling your story is, you may want to have this part of the presentation span more than one slide. In the example, I use a perceptual map to show that unlike my competitors, who aim for comprehensiveness, I compete on an entirely different value proposition—productivity and flexibility.

Slide 11: Customer Acquisition/Go-to-Market: You have defined the market you are entering and the competitive dynamics therein. However, your audience still knows very little about how you will choose to approach this market. By approach, I mean what tactics and tools your startup will leverage to gain market share. What will your sales and marketing campaign look like, and how will you deploy different channels over the twenty-four months you are projecting?

The *key components* of the customer acquisition slide (figure 9.13) center on a chronological plan to capture market share. It describes what your tactics will be, what tools you will use, and what goals you plan to achieve every quarter or semester. In the Syllaber example in figure 9.13 I split the plan into launch, traction, and growth phases. Within each chronological phase I describe the venture's focus, what tasks will be prioritized to ensure follow-through on the chosen foci, and the results I expect. It is the skeleton of a plan that must believably lead to the financial results that I will convey next.

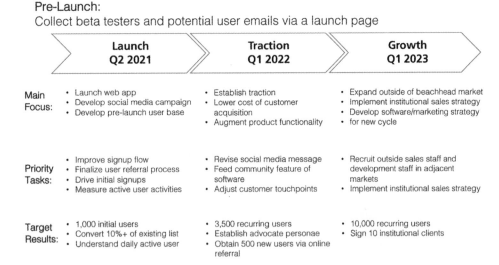

FIGURE 9.13
Customer Acquisition Slide.

9.7   Step 5: Money Matters

Slide 12: Financial Projection: At this point, everyone in the audience should fully understand your idea, its intended market, and the scale of the opportunity. The financial projection slide looks at the financial future of your company if all the assumptions and plans you have drafted thus far pan out. It answers several important questions investors care about, chief of which is how long it will take for this startup to begin making money. In other words, how long will it take for revenues from selling the solution proposed in the earlier slide to overtake startup and ongoing costs? If the combination of the revenue model and cost structure does not make sense, a break-even point will never be reached.

The *key component* of the break-even slide (figure 9.14) is typically a break-even analysis revealing when or at how many units of production (if applicable) the startup will break even. The analysis is sometimes displayed as a graph showing increasing revenue overtaking costs over time. In the sample slide in figure 9.14, I suggest that if everything goes according to plan, Syllaber expects to break even twenty-one months following launch, after signing up 1,900 subscribers. As you know, a lot of work has gone into projecting these numbers, and in most public pitches you likely will not have a chance to or won't choose to go into much more detail. Instead, save all that work for the investor meeting or a question-and-answer session after you deliver your pitch.

9.8   Step 6: Selling a Bright Future

Slide 13: Current Status/Traction: When entrepreneurs refer to traction, they usually mean customer traction (engaged users and paying customers), but traction can also come in

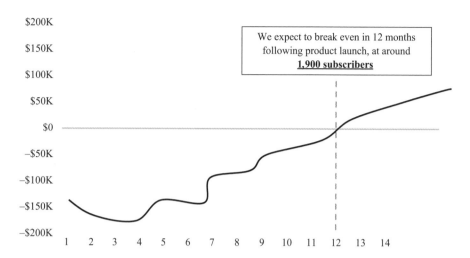

FIGURE 9.14
Break-even Slide.

other forms. Even a small amount of traction means the solution is appealing (to some people), you have figured out how to sell to a customer, and you are tackling a legitimate job to be done.

If your business is not yet operating and you have no evidence of attracting or retaining customers, use this slide to update your audience of the current status of your launch preparations and to demonstrate that you feel confident about hitting milestones (figure 9.15). If you have evidence, which may range from signups, to letters of intent, to actual sales or contracts, tell your audience about it. Doing so will wrap a bow around the business and make it an even more tempting target for investment. However, you should avoid **vanity metrics**, those that may seem to cast your efforts in a positive light but often aren't actionable or verifiably related to anything you can control or repeat in a meaningful way.[11] For example, showing 10,000 total registered accounts might seem impressive, but that number reveals itself to be a vanity metric if there are only 100 active monthly users generating revenue.

Here are some of the *key indicators and actionable metrics* that can advance a case for traction:

- Is your customer base growing aggressively and rapidly based on virality, with little to no paid marketing effort?

- Are you or your business getting a lot of free press? Have you been profiled on cutting-edge industry sites, or has your startup been featured in the popular media?

- Are potential employees or team members coming to you? Does your business have so much appeal that finding talent has more to do with wading through top-tier applicants than convincing folks to apply?

- Are you already profitable or making money?

In the Syllaber slide (see figure 9.15), I highlight three numbers that make the business a safer bet and more interesting to investors. It is important that these numbers match or exceed any goals you laid out in your go-to-market plan.

Slide 14: Ask/Use of Proceeds: As you approach the end of your pitch, you must leave investors or judges clamoring to give you what you need because they truly believe *you* can make it happen and that your business model is not just viable but scalable and exciting (figure 9.16). If you were thorough in your analysis and your business is sound, granting you resources should feel like a no-brainer to a savvy investor. It is time to capitalize on that "I want in" feeling and shamelessly ask for what you need and explain how you would use it if you received it. Note that you should not expect to get investment after delivering a public pitch. Instead, a pitch is a means to getting a private meeting where the fit between an investment fund and a startup can be assessed.

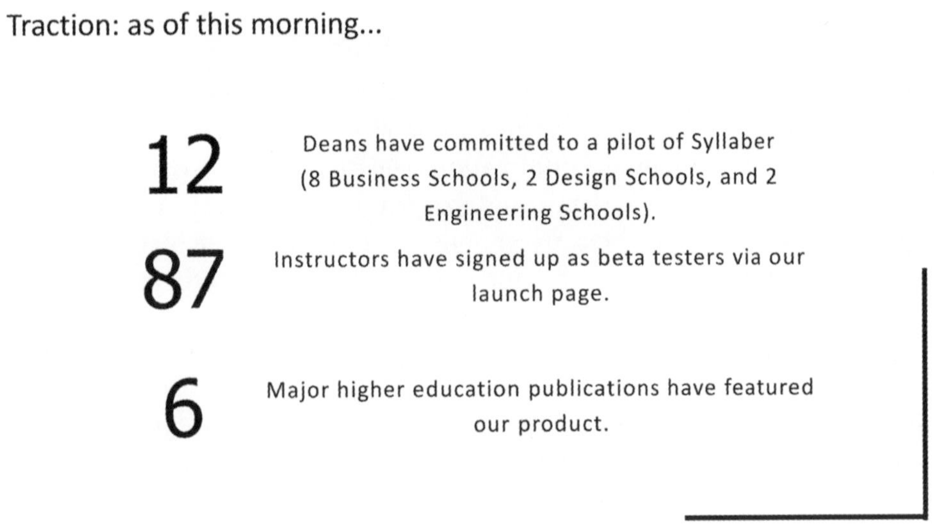

Traction: as of this morning...

12 Deans have committed to a pilot of Syllaber (8 Business Schools, 2 Design Schools, and 2 Engineering Schools).

87 Instructors have signed up as beta testers via our launch page.

6 Major higher education publications have featured our product.

FIGURE 9.15
Traction Slide.

We seek $580k

to launch our sales operation and support product development.

The founding team has contributed $90k.

FIGURE 9.16
Ask Slide.

FIGURE 9.17
Closing Slide.

Slide 15: Final/Closing: While it is acceptable to end your presentation with an ask slide, most founders prefer to add an extra slide to bookend their presentation and provide audience members with important information. The closing slide provides speakers with an opportunity to thank their audience and to open the door for further contact by sharing various contact channels. The key components of the final slide (figure 9.17) include (1) how to contact you directly (e.g., email), (2) ways to learn more about your plans and fundraising requirements (e.g., AngelList profile, company website), and (3) ways to track and engage with the venture or its founding team (e.g., Twitter, Facebook, LinkedIn). In figure 9.17 I try to leverage a minimalist aesthetic to provide all that information without overwhelming the audience. Note that, much like your title slide, this slide will probably remain on view for a long time, so do not make it an afterthought!

9.9   Route Monitoring: Reviewing Your Deck

Now that you have slides that showcase all the major aspects of your business case, I would like you to turn your attention to some aspects of the pitch that most presenters seldom attend to and review your work to identify potential areas for improvement.

- Begin by printing out full-page copies of your slides and laying them out on a large table or taping them to a whiteboard. By laying out your entire deck, you will be able to move the slides around quickly and easily. Using sticky notes, describe the transitions between each of the slides. By transitions I do not mean animations but the phrases you will use to link the slides together. Do the transitions make sense? Would changing slide order improve the narrative flow?

- Some investors may request annotated copies of your slides for review. One way to create annotated slides is to outline a script of what you would typically communicate verbally in the notes or comments sections of programs like PowerPoint, Keynote, or Google slides. Creating these annotations should help you consider what to say during the presentation.

- Take care when sending your materials to third parties. Consider verifying their credentials prior to emailing them a copy of the deck. It would also be prudent to always send your deck in a static format like PDF, to place a semitransparent watermark over each slide, and to indicate who the author of the slides is at the bottom of each slide (e.g., Copyright 20xx. Tim Apple, All Rights Reserved).

- Practicing your delivery in front of a friendly audience is an important step prior to presenting in competition or to investors. Ask supportive individuals who are not afraid to tell you the truth to sit through your presentation and write down comments on how you might improve the presentation. Look for overlap in written comments from your audience members and make sure to address those concerns first. If you do not want to lean on your friends, organizations such as Toastmasters can also help you improve your public speaking and get comfortable delivering your pitch. You can also look for entrepreneur meetups where people regularly discuss their businesses and practice pitching.

- Once entrepreneurs feel ready to pitch, I encourage them to search online for different investor rubrics. These rubrics are typically used by teams of investors (e.g., angel investors, venture capitalists) to systematically evaluate investment opportunities. I push founders to rate their own pitches according to these rubrics. Doing this will give you greater visibility into your strengths and weaknesses. It will let you know what you need to work on next.

9.10   Destination: Reflection and Next Steps

Although it may seem to you that your pitch deck is generally set and all the elements you need to convince investors of the value of your idea are at your fingertips, your deck can and should evolve over time.

- As you present to different audiences, you will start recognizing the questions that keep coming up. By taking note of those questions and adapting the deck to preempt any concerns, you will be able to continuously improve your pitch. Experienced presenters, for instance, have several slides at the ready as addenda to the presentation just in case certain questions get asked. These extra slides could include a deeper dive into unit costs, a slide on partnerships, one on exit possibilities, and many others. Predicting that a judge or investor will ask a question and pulling out a slide perfectly suited to answer the question will set you apart from founders who do not take the time to prepare.

- Almost as important as pitching your own deck is observing pitches across different formats and in different venues. With experience, and after seeing several pitches, you may choose to step away from the boilerplate I presented here and try more creative approaches to pitching. Experienced presenters may flirt with audience interaction, may develop different pitches for different situations (private meetings, conventions), and may even create a video version of the pitch that can be sent to foreign investors. By the time your company has the money it needs to launch, pitching will be second nature and you will have a repertoire of several pitch versions.

· It is sometimes difficult to fully convey the value of your idea during the allotted pitch time, so judges and investors may rely on a question-and-answer session that follows the pitch to clarify doubts and allay concerns. It is up to the founder to answer questions well, and to signal to the audience that they are receptive to advice or "**coachable**."[12‡] Investors and experts want to know that your assumptions are sound and your plan promising, but they understand that even the best plans fall apart sometimes. As such, they want to invest in founders who will listen to reason when the time to pivot comes along.

· Consult the resource page on the MIT Press website (https://mitpress.mit.edu/massa-wild). Content related to this chapter can be found under Founder Resources/Chapter 9.

---

‡ Coachability refers to the degree to which an entrepreneur seeks, carefully considers, and integrates feedback to improve a venture's performance.

Launching Your Startup

Objectives

- Ready your business to receive funding from an external source.
- Ensure that you are legally and financially protected before scaling up your startup.
- Transition from searching for a business model to executing a minimally viable version of your whole venture.

10.1 Mini Case: Launching Pet Krewe

Allison Albert was settled into a flourishing career as a forensic CPA, investigating Ponzi schemes, pursuing class action lawsuits, and untangling the financial complications that follow divorces. Work as a CPA in Denver was packed with challenges and interesting learning experiences at first, but after a while, even the more intricate investigations felt like part of a set routine. Eighty-hour workweeks became a drag on the rest of her life. So, as a break from the daily grind, Allison tried her hand at entrepreneurship by coding a calculator for a multidistrict class action suit, eventually making a good chunk of money by selling it to attorneys in the Gulf South. Working as an entrepreneur—that is, creating and commercializing something new and needed—appealed to Allison, but she was hesitant to put aside all the time and effort she had dedicated to building her accounting skills and reputation, so she went back to work as a CPA.

One week after moving from Denver to New Orleans with her husband in March 2015, Allison was run over by a drunk driver. Facing a traumatic experience, she reevaluated her priorities. Instead of asking herself what the next step in her career should be, she began to consider what kind of work would bring her joy. As a little girl going to a Mennonite school in Pennsylvania, Allison was taught how to sew clothes and common household items. Instead of making teapot cozies and cape dresses, however, the young

Allison defied convention by using her hard-earned sewing skills to make something less utilitarian: costumes for pets. She carried those sewing skills and the memories of designing and making costumes that made people smile and their pets look fabulous into adulthood.

While she was recovering from the accident, Allison thought about how she could combine the hobby she had loved since she was a kid and the parts of her career that made her happy. Encouraged by her husband, she decided to see whether she could turn her hobby of pet costuming into a successful startup. In New Orleans, participants in the Krewe of Barkus and Meoux and the Mystic Krewe of Mardi Paw celebrate Carnival every year by designing intricate costumes for their pets and parading them before the world. Inspired by these krewes and their creativity, Allison dug into whether pet costuming was more than a passing fad and whether the pet lover market was big enough to support a new pet costuming business. She found that in 2010, the National Retail Federation had begun tracking how much people were spending on pet costumes.[1] It turns out that, during Halloween alone, people were spending millions on pet costumes. By the time Allison began her research into the industry, pet costumes represented 15 percent of the $3.2 billion spent on all costume sales. Millennials aged twenty-five to thirty-four were the most likely to dress up their pets, often posting different looks online.

While the trends looked good, Allison had to figure out how she could position a company in the pet costuming market. After all, by the time she decided to look into the industry, there were already a lot of pet costumes available for sale online and in retail outlets. Most of the market share was taken by Rubie's, a family-owned company, founded in 1950, that is the world's largest designer, manufacturer, and distributor of costumes not only for pets but for people. Allison knew that to survive in a market dominated by a giant, she would need to stand out and find a niche. She could not compete on cost because Rubie's size allowed it to produce costumes at higher volumes and ultimately at a lower cost than Allison could as a startup. Like any good forensic investigator, Allison began to look for weaknesses in Rubie's armor. While customers loved the wide selection Rubie's offered and the costumes' affordable prices, a significant chunk of Rubie's online customers complained about the quality of the costumes. Pets, after all, can be rough on costumes, and, in many cases, people complained that the costumes they bought could only be used once. Another issue was comfort. Existing pet costumes did not fit well and made it difficult for even the most well-tempered dog to stand still—a big issue for Instagrammers encouraging their pets to pose for photos.

Insights derived from this research and from dozens of customer interviews with pet owners and operators of stores that sold pet costumes were leading Allison in some interesting directions. It was only a matter of time before Allison came up with the value propositions that would guide Pet Krewe: Instead of making a wide variety of costumes on the cheap, Pet Krewe would focus on quality and comfort, backed by a generous return policy and local production. She began by selling a *minimum viable product*: a lion mane costume that had few moving parts and that she thought would sell well based on her research. Moreover, to make sure every costume designed was commercialized successfully, Allison was going to keep her fingers on the pulse of customers: she tracked pet-related social media accounts on Pinterest and Instagram, conducted keyword searches, and regularly scheduled customer interviews to make sure there was real interest in every product that went into production.

A key determinant of her successful launch was advice she received from experts with startup experience, as well as from strangers she met on airplanes. People she talked to about her business gave her business plan templates, advised her on how to adjust the business to fit new challenges, and kept her informed. She immersed herself in every professional and hobby community she ran into and made them feel like they were a part of her success. Her engagement with her customers and her willingness to build on her own expertise by seeking out advice made her small company a well-tuned disruptor. As Allison likes to note, the growth Pet Krewe has seen has exceeded all of her projections: "We went from twenty-two retail customers in 2018 and will finish 2019 with close to 800 retail outlets. We are projecting 2020 to finish with 6,000 retail outlets and an incredible direct-to-consumer program. I've hired two additional people to help with the accounts, with the focus always being on the customer."

10.2   Orientation: The Launch-Ready Startup

Many founders struggle with knowing when to launch their startup and how to go about doing so. After all, a launch feels like, and in some ways is, an irreversible step that may leave startups exposed to risks they did not foresee. In this book, you have taken important steps to lessen the leap of faith required of you, your founding team, and the funders you have invited along for the ride. Validation of the opportunity you are pursuing and the solution you have devised should, if you took the process seriously, assuage many worries. It is true that many startups fail.[2]* Many of these failed startups launch when they do not have a clear path to viability and or when they understand very little about the markets they are entering. Other startups "build the plane while trying to fly it" and are forced to do all the work you have already done while raising money and executing a sales plan. If you followed the steps in this book, you should not find yourself in that position.

In this final chapter, we review a handful of tasks you should attend to before committing to a launch date for your startup. The steps outlined below are not comprehensive and

---

*Accurate numbers on how many startups fail are notoriously hard to find, partly because definitions of failure vary. According to Shikar Ghosh of the Harvard Business School, if failure means asset liquidation, with investors losing most or all the money they put into the company, then the failure rate for startups is 30 to 40 percent. If, however, failure refers to failing to see the projected return on investment, then the failure rate is 70 to 80 percent. And if failure is defined as declaring a projection and then falling short of meeting it, then the failure rate is a whopping 90 to 95 percent. Carmen Nobel, "Why Companies Fail—and How Their Founders Can Bounce Back," *Research & Ideas*, March 7, 2011, https://hbswk.hbs.edu/item/why-companies-failand-how-their-founders-can-bounce-back.

may vary depending on the type of organization you are launching. We will not get into industry-specific practices (such as stress tests for software or pop-ups for restaurant concepts) but focus instead on general practices followed by successful startups. It is the job of the founder to consider these practices and decide which are appropriate for their venture.

10.3   Step 1: Going Legal

Starting a business can be both exhilarating and stressful. As you work diligently to get your business off the ground, it is important to realize what legal factors need to be considered. Though legal considerations may be initially overlooked or avoided, attending to prelaunch legal requirements is an essential step. Doing legal due diligence upfront and planning for the worst can save your startup a lot of time and money and ensure that the momentum you have been building is not sapped by legal hurdles. Let us explore some of the factors that startups need to consider and why obtaining legal counsel can be beneficial when working through these considerations. A caveat before we begin: the material presented here is intended for general information purposes only and does not constitute legal advice. For legal issues that arise, the reader should always consult qualified legal counsel.

- *Clarity with Cofounders and Team Members.* When your startup involves multiple founding team members, things can get complicated. It is important to make a clear deal with your cofounders, and put it in writing, to avoid ownership conflicts. It is also important, even if it is not something anyone wants to think about, to spell out how an owner's equity position will be dissolved when they want or are forced to exit the venture (i.e., a founder's agreement). It is also wise to begin drawing up a simplified version of what will eventually become your venture's **capitalization table.**[†] Specialized legal counsel and a financial adviser can work in concert to help your startup legally define the founders' roles and responsibilities, salaries, percentage of ownership in the business, cash or assets invested or contributed, and incentive structures.

- *Establish a Business Legal Structure.* Launching a business means you need to decide what sort of entity you want to run in the eyes of the government. The type of business legal structure you choose will depend primarily on three key considerations: liability, taxation, and record-keeping. If you feel that you need to be insulated from legal *liability*, you may choose to avoid sole proprietorships and partnership forms because they do not offer the same level of legal protection that a corporation does. More *tax* options, as well as the ability to issue stock to a broad range of investor types, are also available to corporations. Double taxation, a common disadvantage often

---

[†]The capitalization table (or cap table) is a breakdown of shareholders' equity, including current valuation and ownership split. A basic capitalization table lists each type of equity ownership capital, the individual investors, and issued share prices. A more complex version of a cap table may also include details on potential new funding sources, mergers and acquisitions, public offerings, and so forth.

associated with incorporation, can be avoided with S corporation status wherein business losses can help reduce personal tax liability, particularly in the early years after a company's founding. Keep in mind, however, that corporate forms may have onerous *record-keeping* requirements and may be more expensive to set up. Finally, many small businesses choose to become limited liability corporations (LLCs) because LLCs enjoy some benefits of corporations without the onerous record-keeping. Moreover, in LLCs, profits and losses can be passed through to owners without taxation of the business itself, even as owners are shielded from personal liability. Legal counsel or venture support organizations, such as SCORE, business incubators, or local arms of the Small Business Administration, can help you understand the ins and outs of each business legal structure and align your goals and needs with it.

- *Intellectual Property Protection.* As soon as you start taking steps to incorporate, obtain state or federal licenses, or to have a third party manufacture a product, you should identify which aspects of your business and products are protectable from unfair competition or copycats by different forms of intellectual property protection. Intellectual property protection may apply to trademarks, patents, copyrights, service marks, trade secrets, assignment agreements for employees, and confidentiality agreements. Your legal counsel will need to conduct a **conflict search**‡ to determine whether anyone else already has exclusive claims to the brand names, products, or processes you want to develop. If your venture is built around a solution that is generally unmatched by other businesses, getting intellectual property protection may be crucial to protecting your foothold. Recall that "building a moat" might be a viable strategy to pursue when entering a market. By eschewing legal protection, you are opening the door for third parties to infringe on your intellectual property, with no legal repercussions.

  Note that only truly innovative solutions qualify for patent protection, and certain things that may make your solution stand out, such as shape or design, usually cannot be trademarked. If you plan to commercialize a variation on a commonly available product, then, restricting others from selling the same type of product may not be possible. Nevertheless, you make your contribution stand out by developing a trademark-eligible name for your product, registering the trademark, and always using that trademark name in your marketing and product packaging. Remember, when it comes to intellectual property protection it is always better to be proactive and consult an attorney early in the process than to have to make defensive moves in the future when your ideas are infringed upon.

- *Getting Ahead of Tax Issues.* Getting counsel on important tax issues can save your venture from unnecessary stress and complications. Some tax issues that should be considered are sales tax, payroll tax, stock option issuance, and more. Taxes are an inevitable and necessary part of operating a business and getting legal counsel can help you understand some of the complex issues that come with it.

---

‡In the United States, a conflict search should include a fine-toothed sweep of the U.S. Patent & Trademark Office's (USPTO's) searchable database, or, for copyrights, the U.S. Copyright Office's searchable public catalog.

10.4   Step 2: Preparing to Impress

Launching your solution and generating media and investor buzz can quickly lead to a lot of attention. Most first-time founders have never had a magnifying glass focused so closely on different aspects of their private and professional life before. Before stepping into the spotlight, consider looking in the mirror:

• Create a social media presence that is both impressive and squeaky clean. Some founders choose to completely exit social media, but the total lack of a social media presence may also be a red flag for investors. Delete any photographs you would not want your grandma, rabbi, or high school rival to see, even if they are private. Search for yourself and your team members on Google to ensure that nothing too interesting comes up.

• Spruce up your LinkedIn, AngelList, and Crunchbase profiles. You need to look like a social media–savvy founder who is connected to all the right people and has the right experience to lead a scalable enterprise. Build your connections with industry experts and make sure your team members do the same. Ask yourself this: If you were an angel investor or a venture capitalist, would you invest in yourself? In your founding team members?

• Craft a launch message that you will be sending to your professional contacts, ranging from the experts you spoke with to validate your idea to your college alumni relations office. Make this message warm and hopeful. Do not forget to tell them about your solution and your launch date. Always ask for their help and support! Make it easy for them to get the word out to their networks by creating a shareable video, brochure, or text. Change your email signature to reflect your new status as a founder if you have not done so already.

10.5   Step 3: Reaching Out to Investors (or Not)

When it is time to start establishing relationships with potential investors, you need to find the ones that care about your industry, space, or idea. Some angel funds or venture capitalists are interested in companies of a certain size, some specialize in early-stage or seed funding rounds, and others may focus on a certain sector (e.g., health care) or type of founder (e.g., women). Identifying and getting the attention of the right investor may be one of the most important challenges you will face as a founder. Here are a few pieces of advice that may help you as you navigate investor outreach:

• *Know Your Investor.* Before taking money from, even before meeting with, an investor, do some due diligence. Good investors or investment entities (e.g., angel groups, venture capital funds, family funds) share some key characteristics, which include the following: (1) they are part of a *network* of other investors and experts who may be useful to your venture in the future;[3] (2) they have a solid *reputation* for investing in successful startups,[§] which can be ascertained by looking at their track record and having con-

---

[§]Different early-stage investors have different ways of measuring success. Many tally successes by the profitability of **exits**—ways of "cashing out" an investment. Examples of exits include acquisition by a larger player

versations with people they have worked with; (3) they have enough *capital* to support your current ask and potentially contribute more with future infusions of capital;⁋ and (4) their *style* fits with how you and your team work. Note that some investors are very keen on keeping close tabs on progress while others are more hands-off, some are more comfortable with long-term plays while others like to see tangible results in the short term. Conflict between founders and investors can become a severe hindrance to a startup and can lead to stifled innovation,[4] so take the compatibility factor seriously. Always remember that you are shopping for investors and that reputable investors will expect you to do some vetting. They will typically see such research as a good sign and the mark of a reliable future CEO.

- *Craft Your Outreach.* Investor outreach works in much the same way as reaching out to potential employers except that there are no job listings out there to tell you what investors wish to fund. You will have to figure out each potential investor's profile by digging into what they have funded in the past and determining what might be on their radar now. You can start this discovery process by looking up their portfolio on their fund website or searching AngelList and Crunchbase for the kinds of startups they have funded. Try to understand what these startups had in common when they were funded, what kind of pitch the founders used, and what kind of team they had in place. It is likely that the information available online will be incomplete, but at least you will have a better understanding of who you are about to be in business with. The better your research, the better your rationale for contacting an investor will be. The ideal situation would be if you could be introduced by a third party—such as another investor or expert—that the investor trusts to filter out bad deals or to scout promising founders.[5]

- *Get Your Materials Ready.* Once you contact investors, things may move quickly, so it is a good idea to have certain materials ready for prime time. These include (1) a *one-page summary* that contains only the most critical information about your company and that entices the investor to ask for more; (2) *two versions of your slide deck*, one that you will be presenting and another that is annotated and understandable without you being present to explain; and (3) *financial information,* which should include at least a financial projection and a capitalization table. You might not be asked for all these materials or you may be asked for more—investors have very different styles and expectations, so the key is to overprepare and deliver what is asked for whenever possible.

- *Build Relationships.* Venture capitalists and angel investors have vast networks and know a lot of startups across industries. Founders can sometimes look at an investment round as transactional, but a great relationship with your investors can deliver

---

in a business they invested in, getting bought out of an equity position by a higher-tier investor, and, in very few cases, an initial public offering (IPO).

⁋ Availability of capital may depend on how old a fund is or how much a fund allocates to each investment. Sometimes this information is public, sometimes it is not.

rewards beyond financial support.[6] Tap into their industry knowledge and advice as you grow your business and make them trusted advisers. They can help with talent identification, business modeling, and partnerships, and may even advocate for you in future funding rounds. Do not miss this chance by treating your relationship as if it were a cash-for-equity exchange.

- *Ask for What You Need.* Founders often fret over how much money to ask for from investors. Taking money early on before you have had time to validate a solution can put undue pressure on your startup and set unrealistic expectations. Once you know how much you will need based on your calculations, try to scenario plan for worst- and best-case scenarios by playing with your numbers. Try to understand the levers that may influence the trajectory of the venture and use those to build out comfortable milestones. Experienced investors will want to hear your thoughts and help you set ambitious yet achievable milestones that will please everyone in the room.[7] Be wary of investors who are willing to invest in you before you have shown a realistic plan with reasonable milestones and some traction—they may have incompatible expectations, lack the right kind of experience, and be more trouble than they are worth. Also, keep in mind that in a study of over 200 startups that raised over $360 million, Tom Eisenmann discovered that founders need an average of forty investor meetings and about twelve weeks to close a round.[8] Given the length of time you will likely need to raise money, my suggestion is that you bide your time, tread carefully, and do your best to make informed decisions.

10.6   Step 4: Preparing for Launch Day

As you get ready to open your doors, introduce your app, launch your website, or all those things, consider the significance of this moment. Startups typically launch only once. And launch days are exciting not just for the stakeholders involved but for the whole community. Here are a few fun things you can do:

- Once you are done cleaning up your own act, make sure you do the same for your venture. A press kit available via the company website should contain all the information bloggers, business journalists, and trade publication writers need to write a compelling story about your journey. Include information about your solution and customer experiences with your solution. Share your personal bio, include high-resolution images of you and your solution, along with well-designed, sharp-looking brand logos. Create a press release that links readers back to your press kit. You may be surprised at the amount of traffic and customer interest an old-fashioned press release can garner.

- Have a suitable, affordable launch party to thank the people who have helped you get this far. The party can also serve an announcement to your community that you are now open to having conversations about investment, hiring, and other activities reserved for startup founders. Do not forget to invite the mayor, and publicly thank your significant others and family members who have supported you on your journey. Prepare everyone for the next round of exciting developments and keep them on the edge of their seats!

10.7 Destination: Reflection

Congratulations on completing your journey through this book! Doing so took dedication and a great deal of effort. Know that by approaching the entrepreneurial process systematically, you are better prepared than most early-stage founders. This does not mean you can stop learning or that the journey is over. Receiving funding from investors or even achieving financial break-even status are just the first few milestones on the path. Look forward to scaling up your startup, growing your team, and acing the transition from founder to CEO.

Notes

Welcome

1. J. Robert Baum and Edwin A. Locke, "The Relationship of Entrepreneurial Traits, Skill, and Motivation to Subsequent Venture Growth," *Journal of Applied Psychology* 89, no. 4 (2004): 587.

2. Joseph C. Picken, "From Founder to CEO: An Entrepreneur's Roadmap," *Business Horizons* 60, no. 1 (2017): 7–14.

3. Olav Sorenson and Toby E. Stuart, "12 Entrepreneurship: A Field of Dreams?," *Academy of Management Annals* 2, no. 1 (2008): 517–543.

4. Einar A. Rasmussen and Roger Sørheim, "Action-Based Entrepreneurship Education," *Technovation* 26, no. 2 (2006): 185–194.

5. On wayfinding, see Paul Arthur and Romedi Passini, *Wayfinding: People, Signs, and Architecture* (New York: McGraw-Hill, 1992). On startup ecosystems, see Erik Stam, "Entrepreneurial Ecosystems and Regional Policy: A Sympathetic Critique," *European Planning Studies* 23, no. 9 (2015): 1759–1769.

6. Steve Case, *The Third Wave: An Entrepreneur's Vision of the Future* (New York: Simon & Schuster, 2017).

7. Brad Feld, *Startup Communities: Building an Entrepreneurial Ecosystem in Your City* (Hoboken, NJ: John Wiley & Sons, 2012).

8. Timothy Bates, William E. Jackson III, and James H. Johnson Jr., "Advancing Research on Minority Entrepreneurship," *Annals of the American Academy of Political and Social Science* 613, no. 1 (2007): 10–17.

Chapter 1

1. Michael J. Swenson, Gary K. Rhoads, and David B. Whitlark, "Finding and Developing New Product Ideas: An Ideation Process for Entrepreneurs," *Journal of Applied Business and Economics* 15, no. 3 (2013): 19–25.

2. Ranjay Galuti, "Five Sources of Startup Ideas," *Harvard Business* Review, 2013, https://hbr.org /2013/11/five-sources-of-start-up-ideas.

3. Paul Graham, "How to Get Startup Ideas," November 2012, http://www.paulgraham.com /startupideas.html.

4. Marily Oppezzo and Daniel L. Schwartz, "Give Your Ideas Some Legs: The Positive Effect of Walking on Creative Thinking," *Journal of Experimental Psychology: Learning, Memory, and Cognition* 40, no. 4 (2014): 1142.

5. Steven Johnson, *Where Good Ideas Come From: The Natural History of Innovation* (New York: Penguin, 2011).

6. Paul Paulus, "Groups, Teams, and Creativity: The Creative Potential of Idea-Generating Groups," *Applied Psychology* 49, no. 2 (2000): 237–262.

7. Steve Blank and Bob Dorf, *The Startup Owner's Manual: The Step-by Step Guide for Building a Great Company* (Hoboken, NJ: John Wiley & Sons, 2020).

8. Clayton Christensen, Taddy Hall, Karen Dillon, and David Scott Duncan, *"Competing against Luck": The Story of Innovation and Customer Choice* (New York: HarperCollins, 2016).

9. Alexander Ardichvili, Richard Cardozo, and Sourav Ray, "A Theory of Entrepreneurial Opportunity Identification and Development," *Journal of Business Venturing* 18, no. 1 (2003): 105–123.

10. Moon Youngme Moon, "Uber: Changing the Way the World Moves," *Harvard Business Publishing*, Case 101 (2015).

11. Bill Aulet, *Disciplined Entrepreneurship: 24 Steps to a Successful Startup* (Hoboken, NJ: John Wiley & Sons, 2013).

12. Seth Godin, *Purple Cow, New Edition: Transform Your Business by Being Remarkable* (New York: Penguin, 2009).

13. Bobby J. Calder, "Writing a Brand Positioning Statement and Translating It into Brand Design," *Kellogg on Marketing* (2012): 92–111.

Chapter 2

1. E. Prandelli, M. Pasquini, and G. Verona, "In User's Shoes: An Experimental Design on the Role of Perspective Taking in Discovering Entrepreneurial Opportunities," *Journal of Business Venturing* 31 (2016): 287–301.

2. Jagdish N. Sheth, Rajendra S. Sisodia, and Arun Sharma, "The Antecedents and Consequences of Customer-centric Marketing," *Journal of the Academy of marketing Science* 28, no. 1 (2000): 55–66.

3. Sussie C. Morrish, Morgan P. Miles, and Jonathan H. Deacon, "Entrepreneurial Marketing: Acknowledging the Entrepreneur and Customer-centric Interrelationship," *Journal of Strategic Marketing* 18, no. 4 (2010): 303–316.

4. Alexandra Samuel, "Psychographics Are Just As Important for Marketers As Demographics," *Harvard Business Review*, March 2016, https://hbr.org/2016/03/psychographics-are-just-as-important -for-marketers-asdemographics.

5. Bryan Lilly and Tammy R. Nelson, "Fads: Segmenting the Fad-Buyer Market," *Journal of Consumer Marketing* 20, no. 3 (2003): 252–265.

Chapter 3

1. Scott A. Shane, *The Illusions of Entrepreneurship: The Costly Myths That Entrepreneurs, Investors, and Policy Makers Live By* (New Haven, CT: Yale University Press, 2008).

2. Dimo Dimov, "Beyond the Single-Person, Single-Insight Attribution in Understanding Entrepreneurial Opportunities," *Entrepreneurship Theory and Practice* 31, no. 5 (2007): 713–731.

3. Theodore Levitt, "What Business Are You In? Classic Advice from Theodore Levitt," *Harvard Business Review* 84, no. 10 (2006): 126–137.

4. Gavin Cassar, "Industry and Startup Experience on Entrepreneur Forecast Performance in New Firms," *Journal of Business Venturing* 29, no. 1 (2014): 137–151.

5. Frédéric Delmar and Scott Shane, "Does Experience Matter? The Effect of Founding Team Experience on the Survival and Sales of Newly Founded Ventures," *Strategic Organization* 4, no. 3 (2006): 215–247.

6. Robert V. Kozinets, Kristine De Valck, Andrea C. Wojnicki, and Sarah J. S. Wilner, "Networked Marratives: Understanding Word-of-Mouth Marketing in Online Communities," *Journal of Marketing* 74, no. 2 (2010): 71–89.

7. Jonah Berger and Eric M. Schwartz, "What Drives Immediate and Ongoing Word of Mouth?," *Journal of Marketing Research* 48, no. 5 (2011): 869–880.

8. Emanuel Rosen, *The Anatomy of Buzz Revisited: Real-Life Lessons in Word-of-Mouth Marketing* (New York: Doubleday, 2009).

9. Steve Blank, *The Four Steps to the Epiphany: Successful Strategies for Products That Win* (Hoboken, NJ: John Wiley & Sons, 2020), 30.

10. Milagros Castillo-Montoya, "Preparing for Interview Research: The Interview Protocol Refinement Framework," *Qualitative Report* 21, no. 5 (2016).

Chapter 4

1. Marc de Swaan Arons, Frank van den Driest, and Keith Weed, "The Ultimate Marketing Machine," *Harvard Business Review* 92, no. 7 (2014): 54–63.

2. Anirudh Dhebar, "Toward a Compelling Customer Touchpoint Architecture," *Business Horizons* 56, no. 2 (2013): 199–205.

3. Alistair Cockburn, *Writing Effective Use Cases* (Upper Saddle River, NJ: Addison-Wesley, 2000.

Chapter 5

1. Christoph Zott and Raphael Amit, "Business Model Design and the Performance of Entrepreneurial Firms," *Organization Science* 18, no. 2 (2007): 181–199.

2. Jeffrey Pfeffer, "Producing Sustainable Competitive Advantage through the Effective Management of People," *Academy of Management Perspectives* 9, no. 1 (1995): 55–69.

3. Alexander Osterwalder and Yves Pigneur, *Business Model Generation: A Handbook for Visionaries, Game Changers, and Challengers* (Hoboken, NJ: John Wiley & Sons, 2010).

4. IDEO, *Human-Centered Design Toolkit* (2009), https://www.ideo.com/work/human-centered-design -toolkit.

5. Bert Rosenbloom, *Marketing Channels* (Cengage Learning, 2012).

6. Chai Lee Goi, "A Review of Marketing Mix: 4Ps or More?," *International Journal of Marketing Studies* 1, no. 1 (2009): 2.

Chapter 6

1. Steve Blank and Bob Dorf, *The Startup Owner's Manual: The Step-by-Step Guide for Building a Great Company* (Hoboken, NJ: John Wiley & Sons, 2020).

2. Paul J. H. Schoemaker, "How to Link Strategic Vision to Core Capabilities," *Sloan Management Review* 34 (1992): 67–67.

3. W. Chan Kim and Renée Mauborgne, *Blue Ocean Strategy, expanded edition: How to Create Uncontested market space and Make the Competition Irrelevant* (Boston: Harvard Business Press, 2014).

4. Joshua Gans, E.L. Scott, and S. Stern, "Strategy for Start-ups," *Harvard Business Review*, May–June 2018, 44–51.

5. Fernand Gobet, Peter C. R. Lane, Steve Croker, Peter C. H. Cheng, Gary Jones, Iain Oliver, and Julian M. Pin, "Chunking Mechanisms in Human Learning," *Trends in Cognitive Sciences* 5, no. 6 (2001): 236–243.

6. Chiranjeev S. Kohli and Lance Leuthesser, "Product Positioning: A Comparison of Perceptual Mapping Techniques," *Journal of Product & Brand Management* 42, no. 4 (1993): 10–19.

7. Harvey Carruthers, "Using PEST Analysis to Improve Business Performance," *In Practice* 31, no. 1 (2009): 37–39.

Chapter 7

1. Dobrila Rancic Moogk, "Minimum Viable Product and the Importance of Experimentation in Technology Startups," *Technology Innovation Management Review* 2, no. 3 (2012).

2. Dan Siroker and Pete Koomen, *A/B Testing: The Most Powerful Way to Turn Clicks into Customers* (Hoboken, NJ: John Wiley & Sons, 2013).

3. Giff Constable, *Testing with Humans* (Giff Constable, 2018).

4. Chris Spiek, "Unpacking the Progress Making Forces Diagram," *#JTBD* (blog), February 23, 2012, http://jobstobedone.org/radio/unpacking-the-progress-making-forces-diagram.

Chapter 8

1. Minet Schindehutte and Michael H. Morris, "Pricing as Entrepreneurial Behavior," *Business Horizons* 44, no. 4 (2001): 41–48.

2. Gavin Cassar, "Financial Statement and Projection Preparation in Start-up Ventures," *Accounting Review* 84, no. 1 (2009): 27–51.

3. Gilad Livne, Ana Simpson, and Eli Talmor, "Do Customer Acquisition Cost, Retention and Usage Matter to Firm Performance and Valuation?," *Journal of Business Finance & Accounting* 38, no. 3–4 (2011): 334–363.

4. Paul Farris, Neil Bendle, Phillip E. Pfeifer, and David Reibstein, *Marketing Metrics: The Manager's Guide to Measuring Marketing Performance* (New York: FT Press, 2015).

Chapter 9

1. Jeffrey M. Pollack, Matthew W. Rutherford, and Brian G. Nagy, "Preparedness and Cognitive Legitimacy as Antecedents of New Venture Funding in Televised Business Pitches," *Entrepreneurship Theory and Practice* 36, no. 5 (2012): 915–939.

2. Christoph Zott and Quy Nguyen Huy, "How Entrepreneurs Use Symbolic Management to Acquire Resources," *Administrative Science Quarterly* 52, no. 1 (2007): 70–105.

3. Mantonakis, Antonia, Pauline Rodero, Isabelle Lesschaeve, and Reid Hastie. "Order in Choice: Effects of Serial Position on Preferences," *Psychological Science* 20, no. 11 (2009): 1309–1312.

4. Danziger, Shai, Jonathan Levav, and Liora Avnaim-Pesso, "Extraneous Factors in Judicial Decisions." *Proceedings of the National Academy of Sciences* 108, no. 17 (2011): 6889–6892.

5. Sidney G. Winter, "The Satisficing Principle in Capability Learning," *Strategic Management Journal* 21, no. 10–11 (2000): 981–996.

6. Don A. Moore, "Order Effects in Preference Judgments: Evidence for Context Dependence in the Generation of Preferences." *Organizational Behavior and Human Decision Processes* 78, no. 2 (1999): 146–165.

7. Scott Shane, Will Drover, David Clingingsmith, and Moran Cerf, "Founder Passion, Neural Engagement and Informal Investor Interest in Startup Pitches: An fMRI Study," *Journal of Business Venturing* 35, no. 4 (2020), article 105949.

8. Kimberly D. Elsbach and Roderick M. Kramer. "Assessing Creativity in Hollywood Pitch Meetings: Evidence for a Dual-Process Model of Creativity Judgments," *Academy of Management Journal* 46, no. 3 (2003): 283–301.

9. Rüdiger F. Pohl, ed., *Cognitive Illusions: Intriguing Phenomena in Thinking, Judgment and Memory* (New York: Routledge/Taylor & Francis, 2016).

10. Brian G. Nagy, Jeffrey M. Pollack, Matthew W. Rutherford, and Franz T. Lohrke, "The Influence of Entrepreneurs' Credentials and Impression Management Behaviors on Perceptions of New Venture Legitimacy," *Entrepreneurship Theory and Practice* 36, no. 5 (2012): 941–965.

11. Diana Kander, *All in Startup: Launching a New Idea When Everything Is on the Line* (Hoboken, NJ: John Wiley & Sons, 2014).

12. Michael P. Ciuchta, Chaim Letwin, Regan Stevenson, Sean McMahon, and M. Nesij Huvaj, "Betting on the Coachable Entrepreneur: Signaling and Social Exchange in Entrepreneurial Pitches," *Entrepreneurship Theory and Practice* 42, no. 6 (2018): 860–885.

Chapter 10

1. Prosper Insights & Analytics, "National Retail Federation Annual Survey," 2008, https://nrf.com/tag/pet-costumes.

2. Carmen Nobel, "Why Companies Fail—and How Their Founders Can Bounce Back," *Working Knowledge: Business Ideas for Business Leaders,* Harvard Business School, 2011, https://hbswk.hbs.edu/item/why-companies-failand-how-their-founders-can-bounce-back.

3. Sea Jin Chang, "Venture Capital Financing, Strategic Alliances, and the Initial Public Offerings of Internet Startups," *Journal of Business Venturing* 19, no. 5 (2004): 721–741.

4. Veroniek Collewaert and Harry J. Sapienza. "How Does Angel Investor–Entrepreneur Conflict Affect Venture Innovation? It Depends," *Entrepreneurship Theory and Practice* 40, no. 3 (2016): 573–597.

5. Annalisa Croce, Francesca Tenca, and Elisa Ughetto, "How Business Angel Groups Work: Rejection Criteria in Investment Evaluation," *International Small Business Journal* 35, no. 4 (2017): 405–426.

6. Scott Shane and Daniel Cable, "Network Ties, Reputation, and the Financing of New Ventures," *Management Science* 48, no. 3 (2002): 364–381.

7. W. R. Kerr, J. Lerner, and A. Schoar, "The Consequences of Entrepreneurial Finance: Evidence from Angel Financings," *Review of Financial Studies,* 27, no. 1 (2014): 20–55.

8. Tom Eisenmann. "What We Learned from 200 Startups Who Raised $360M," *Docsend.com,* https://docsend.com/view/p8jxsqr.

Index